Isaiah 40:31

*Tethered
to an
Unwavering
God
in the
Heights*

HOPE

*Tethered
to an
Unwavering
God
in the
Depths*

DEDICATION

To the brave women of "Hope" who have courageously shared their stories with you:

You all stand among the heroes of my faith. You all shine so brightly in such a dark world. You all have deposited such hope in my heart, and I am confident that your stories will bring hope and freedom to more hearts than any of us could fathom.

Lindsay, Jessica, Kristin, Lindsay, Sue, Lori, Taylor, Bristi, and Cassie:

I am so honored to call each one of you a friend and a sister in Christ. Your faith in Jesus has made mine stronger. Whatever the enemy intended for evil in each of your lives, God has so faithfully used for good. He is so glorified through your stories. Thank you for sharing them with the world.

HEIGHTS

DEPTHS

ABOUT THE AUTHOR

Cherie Wagner's life-long passion is two-fold: knowing Jesus Christ and making Him known. Author of *Found On My Knees*, *Awake O Sleeper*, and *Rest*, Cherie writes Bible studies and books for women that will encourage them to know and believe God's Word, equip them to live it, and empower them to take it and transform this generation for Jesus Christ. Cherie, her husband Jeremy, and their son Redford live in Mesa, Arizona where they are actively involved in the ministries of Central Christian Church. Born and raised in Chicago and transplanted to the desert of Arizona, Cherie is a city girl at heart with a wild love for the mountains. A coffee connoisseur, a lover of knowledge, and forever a student of God's Word, she loves life and tries to live it to the fullest. Connect with Cherie at **NeueThing.org**.

FOREWORD

In every stage of our lives, hope blooms back another layer of our hearts and begins to teach us what it looks like to balance strong desire and confident expectation with the reality of living in a disappointing world. It's different for each of us, of course, but we all grow up experiencing this process in various stages. When we're children, we hope Santa receives our Christmas wish list in time to make any necessary adjustments to his sleigh load. In our senior year of high school, we hope to do well enough on exams that we get accepted into our college of choice. As we mature, we hope that sooner than later we'll find the love of our lives. We hope for an exciting, fulfilling job we can be successful at. We hope to make enough money to support our aging parents or growing children. We hope to survive the recently diagnosed disease we didn't see coming.

The outcome of each of those events can truly make or break both our hearts and the way we approach the next time we might possibly even think about "getting our hopes up." As Proverbs 13:12 (ESV) puts it, "Hope deferred makes the heart sick, but a desire fulfilled is a tree of life." Exactly. Hope realized produces more hope. Hope dashed, and our once unshakeable optimism can find itself in an identity crisis.

The truth is, the longer we reside on this spinning globe, the more we experience anticipation deflated and hearts broken, and eventually, we must decide whether or not we will move forward choosing hope. Sometimes, this decision comes in the valley when we push past the feeling of foolishness to reach for the glimmer of hope-against-hope that we won't stay in this present season forever—courageously peeking through our squinted eyes against the darkness to catch the spark of dawn. Sometimes we choose it while climbing up the side of the impossible mountain, determined to push through adversity and struggle on, and choosing to hold on to the possibility that we might … just … make it … up. And sometimes, we arrive at that choice on the peak of our Mt. Everest, reveling in the victory of the summit and resolving to keep hiking forward even though we know inevitably the road will lead us down again. We do this because we believe that goodness and mercy, although not always in a form we immediately recognize, will follow us all the days of our lives.

The author of the book you hold in your hands has been around for the vast majority of hopes both dashed and realized in the past sixteen years of my life. Since we first met freshman year at Moody Bible Institute (pretend you can't do math and don't guess our ages now), she has, without fail, been one of the key people God has used time and again to point (and occasionally drag) me back to hope. She has faithfully done the work of an evangelist in my life—proclaiming the good news of the Gospel over and into every situation we've found ourselves in, good and bad, joyful and sad—and she's done it by reminding me that my hope cannot be in this world. If it is, I'm in trouble, because anyone who's watched the news for over 60 seconds knows this old earth is getting darker by the day, groaning as it waits for Jesus to come make all things new.

Cherie has been faithful to remind me that the only eternally secure anchor I can fix my hope on is the One who holds forever in His hands, the One lovingly carrying us through this thing we call life from our first breath to our final exhale this side of heaven. Because at some point in our lives, we begin to understand that who we ultimately hope in is fundamental to the sustainability of hope.

Cherie has been in the trenches of the hardest, saddest, darkest moments of my adult life, and the reason she continues to be such a trusted voice is because I've been in those same trenches with her on her own journey, and I've seen the way she clings to Jesus like a lifeboat in a hurricane. I've watched her choose faith over fear time and time again. I've heard her whisper belief in the unshakeable promises of God into the deafening silence of doubt and discouragement. And I've seen her recount His goodness, waving tales of His unfailing faithfulness, like a flag, over my crippling fear. Hope. She's clung to hope, she's spoken hope over me, and if you make it past this forward (I promise, I'm almost done. Hang in there!), she will speak it over you, as well.

When you choose hope—whatever stage, season, situation, or circumstance you are in—hope is defiant. It reaches way, way down into the intimidating "not yet" and speaks life into the praying, as you wait and hope for the reality of "now." I'm praying that this book stirs up in your heart a belief that God is working all things together for good, just as He promises us in Romans 8:28, and that you bravely and fiercely attach your hope to the One who will never disappoint: Jesus.

> *Be strong and take heart, all you who hope in the Lord!*
>
> Psalm 31:24

Here's hoping,
Lindsay McCaul

INTRODUCTION

At the close of every calendar year, at least for the past several years, I have found myself reflecting on the previous twelve months and looking forward with expectancy to what the next year will hold. This time of reflection has not always been easy, but it's always proven to be good. It has taught me to live a bit more intentionally and purposefully with the time that has been entrusted to me.

As each year comes to a close, I pray and ask God to give me a word for the upcoming year, a word that will mark me and all that I do for those next twelve months. When the word "hope" began to shine on the horizon of 2016, I did not know why, but I chose to embrace the word and whatever journey awaited me. Faith can be a terrifying thing, don't you think?

The foreknowledge of God is a remarkable thing, and it has proven to be so sweet in my own life as it is realized more fully. Only God could know that I would need to cling to hope in 2016 like I had never been required to before. It was a hard twelve months, but even in the hard, there was so much good to be found. It was a year of new beginnings, new life, and new opportunities, but new isn't always easy.

As my word "hope" began to settle among all of the difficulty that 2016 brought, my vision started to become crystal clear. Every single platform I've ever taken and every book I've written—those messages have all come from places I've been and where I've walked with Jesus. Hope was beginning to shine on what felt like my own hopelessness, and as that truth began to unfold, so did these words.

Say "hello" to the book you hold in your hands. Every word on every page has been a faith-filled journey in which I still find myself. Isn't that just how the Lord works, though? Does He not use our pain for His purposes? Does He not work all things out for the good? These pages and this message of hope are nearer to my heart than you might ever know. I had to learn these truths and come to a place where I believe them to be true for me before I was ever able to write a single one of them for you.

Hope: Tethered To An Unwavering God is an invitation to hope-filled living, whether you already find yourself hopeful or you find yourself in pits of despair. Each chapter highlights a different aspect of what hope does, and it allows you to approach hope from whatever position you are in today. You are welcome to come just as you are. You are invited to sit at the table.

I would encourage each one of you to begin by reading chapters one and six (Hope Is and Hopeless), but after that, you are welcome to jump in to any chapter you wish, in any order that you'd like. Because the message of this book is intended to meet you where you are, it is not necessary that you read it from cover to cover. These two chapters will help to lay a strong foundation of what hope is and what it isn't, but after that, I invite you to engage with these words from whatever place you find yourself. If you are finding yourself in a place of despair, maybe you want to open up to chapter six today. If you are experiencing hope right now, then chapter two might be a great fit for you today.

My primary purpose throughout this book is to prove to you through Scripture that hope can be known and fully experienced in any season of life. It can be known in the darkest of times, and it can be known in the light. When life feels like it's been flipped upside down, hope can still be the anchor for our souls. When all seems to be going smoothly, hope remains our reality. Life will waver, but our God will not. He is our hope, so our footing can remain secure in Him.

Hope is a strong and confident expectation. Hope is an unwavering trust in the unchanging character of God.

If you make it through every page, you will come to know that the above definition is true. Hope is not wishful thinking. Hope is so much more than that. Join me as we, together, learn to live in the reality in which God intended for us to live: Hope.

He did not.

Something I suppose you should know is that while we live in a desert and go much of the year without rainfall, when it does rain, it pours. And when it rains, it can often flood because the ground is so hard from the months of extreme heat and lack of water, that it doesn't quickly absorb the rain. My husband, the former boy scout, was well-versed in all of this, and he was not worried in the least possible way. His idea was simply to keep on going, walking through the muddy water, if necessary, but he was certain and determined that we would not only see the other side of this small lake, but we were going to finish this hike and enjoy it.

On we went, marching through the mud to the beat of adventure. If you know me at all, you know that I don't do mud. I've never been much of a girly girl, most often the tomboy or the athlete, but I do not like to get dirty. Sounds like a contradiction, right? Well, either way, I don't do mud. However, I married an off-roading, Jeep driving, mountain loving, adventurous, bearded man, and despite the fact that all things wilderness are not really my comfort zone, I love him, so on I trudged.

It was only minutes before we began to sink into the mud. My husband had come well-prepared with solid hiking boots. Me? Of course not! I don't own hiking boots. I had on simple tennis shoes that, truth be told, probably weren't even the best option for a hike without mud. As the mud began to fill our shoes, I realized that we had made it to the middle of this little lake, and there really wasn't any turning back now. The same distance that stretched out in front of us was the same distance we had already made it through, so on we went.

It became increasingly difficult, though, to keep walking, as the weight of our now submerged feet grew heavier with each step. So? We took our shoes and socks off. That's right. This city slicker is now marching barefoot through six to twelve inches of wet mud, just **hoping** to make it to the other side. **Hoping**.

Despite my assumptions of how I thought this "adventure" would end, which included missing persons reports among other things, we not only made it to the other side of this mud pit, but we also found a stream in which we washed off our muddy feet, socks, and shoes. We proceeded to put these wet, cold, and somewhat still muddy socks and shoes back on our feet, and we did in fact finish that five mile loop.

Crazy story, right? Maybe not to some of you who would dare to do that and so much more, but for me, all I could do was **hope** that we were going to make it out alive. I know I might sound dramatic, but it felt dramatic. As we kept trudging on while caked in mud, I found myself **hoping**—wishing—that we would get out before the sun went down, before the creatures came out, before we became dinner.

Fast forward a few years to the present. I found myself uncovering a definition of hope that has shifted my perspective on everything. As I look back at that seemingly treacherous hike, in which my husband was confident that we were in no real danger, and even as I reflect further back into the majority of my life, I realize that I held onto an inaccurate definition of the word *hope*. The hope I was desperately trying to cling to on that hike was nothing more than a wish, a desire maybe, but it held no real certainty of fulfillment.

If we are honest with ourselves, I imagine many of us could or would say the same about our own stories of trying to cling onto hope in our seemingly hopeless situations. Perhaps our own hope felt like little more than a wish at times, and because of that, we may have lost our confidence in hope.

Before we move any further into the message of this book, we must begin with an accurate understanding of what hope really is. Hope is not a wish. It's not just a desire. It's far more than a longing, a perceived want, or even need. If it were only those things and nothing more, Scripture would not command us to hope. But, it does. Because it is commanded of us, we can then assume that it is possible to actually possess and maintain real hope. We must lean in a bit further to see what we have been missing.

Hope is a strong and confident expectation. Hope is unwavering trust in the unchanging character of God.

How's that for a starting point? We will spend the rest of this chapter unpacking that definition and allowing this new understanding of hope to reshape and renew our minds. I believe that a false understanding of hope has effectively led far too many of us to live and lead hopeless lives.

No more!

We have an opportunity today to allow Truth to become the loudest voice in our lives. We have an opportunity today to listen less to the voices of this world and instead to listen more to the voice of the Word. We have an opportunity today to move from hopeless living to hope-filled living. It's time to move.

Hope is a strong and confident expectation.

If you and I are ever going to possess and maintain any amount of hope in our lives, we will need to understand what hope isn't and start clinging to what hope is. Hope is not a wish, a want, or a desire. Hope does not leave room for the insecurity that a mere wish, want, or desire can bring. Hope is so much more than that. Hope expects with a sense of strength and confidence. Hope does not waver. Hope is the anchor for our souls.

> *We have this hope as an anchor for the soul, firm and secure.*
>
> Hebrews 6:19a

Think of what an anchor provides for a ship. It helps to secure the vessel in place. It helps prevent the outside elements from moving the ship in a direction it does not wish to go. Now, take that picture and translate it to your life. Hope is your anchor. It secures you in place. It prevents outside elements from moving you in a direction you do not wish to go. This is hope.

Imagine living your life from this perspective as opposed to the faulty understanding of hope that so many of us have tried to hold onto. What a difference this true understanding of hope could bring to our souls! This hope says, "You can remain steady and secure even when your circumstances are not." This hope says, "You can remain strong and confident in the face of the unknown." This hope breeds deeper trust in us.

Hope is unwavering trust in the unchanging character of God.

Now, let's move to the second half of our definition of hope. Notice that the first part had to do with us. This second part has everything to do with God. The first part revealed who we can be when we possess a biblical understanding of hope: strong and confident. This second part reveals the reason why: God is who He says He is.

God's character does not change, even when our circumstances do. Here's another way to say that: Our circumstances will never alter the character of God. Not ever. God remains the same, even when we do not. God is steady, even when we are shifting. God is faithful, even when we are faithless.

> *... if we are faithless, He remains*
> *faithful, for He cannot disown Himself.*
>
> 2 Timothy 2:13

It is because God's character does not change that we can have unwavering trust in Him. Do you see the connection? Hope is the ability to have unwavering trust BECAUSE God's character does not change. Our hope is resting in something secure, not something that wavers. Therefore, we do not need to waver either.

If you find yourself wavering today, unable to possess and maintain hope, might I suggest that perhaps your hope is misplaced? We put hope in all sorts of things. We put hope in desired outcomes. We put hope in the expectations that we place on others. We put hope in success and achievement. We put hope in material possessions. Notice how all of these things are temporal, though. None of these things lasts, not eternally anyway. Also, notice how all of these things leave room for disappointment. The outcomes that we chase often turn out much differently than we wanted them to. Expectations are often not met. Successes and achievements come and go, and the happiness that they can bring is also fleeting. Material possessions always fail to provide lasting joy, yet we still keep putting our hope in them and what they might provide for us.

And we keep coming up short.

As long as our hopes are misplaced, our joy will be also. Jesus is the creator of hope; therefore, He is also the source of hope. He is the provider of hope, and He is the sustainer of hope. Hope is found in Him, and every time we continue to look for hope elsewhere, we will come up short.

I would love to tell you with confidence that there will come a point in time when we don't experience the wavering, shifting, and undesirable circumstances that leave us reeling, but I can't, so I won't. Our lives will continue to waver on this side of heaven because we are not in control of them. Things will continue to happen that will rock our boats and shake our footing, but hope tethers us to an unwavering God. Hope secures us to a God who is not moved by the things that move us. Hope anchors us to steady and solid ground. Hope fixes our gaze on Jesus instead of our circumstances. Hope reminds us of who God is.

This is my hope story.

The year was 2005, I was a senior in college, and hope was on the horizon. I had just spent nearly four years in a pressure cooker of spiritual growth, Bible learning, and Christian community at the Bible college I attended, and I was ready to spread my wings and fly toward all the hopes and dreams I had for my future—a future that included only good things. I was about to graduate with honors. I was a leader on campus. I had the promise of a dream job in ministry. I had the love of a young man. Everything pointed toward a hope-filled future.

There are moments in time that forever freeze frame themselves into your memory—moments that no matter how long ago they were, feel like they happened just yesterday. As my very long, international flight neared its way back to O'Hare airport in Chicago, my sleepy eyes opened to watch what will always be one of my favorite sites: Chicago at night from the sky. I love flying into this city at any time of day, but at night, it holds a rather special beauty to me. It was the middle of the night when the wheels of that plane finally made contact with the ground below. I reached for my phone, which had been off for the past two weeks while I had been in Africa with several of my fellow students, doing short-term missions work there. There were several messages that I determined could wait until morning to respond to because my first priority was to inform my roommate and best friend that I had made it home safely. Our flight had been rerouted while over the Atlantic Ocean, which had caused some concern for those who were awaiting our return, so I dialed her number to quickly assure her that we had in fact made it home, safe and sound.

Nothing, and I mean nothing, could have prepared me for the message she was about to deliver to me on the other end of that call. I can still see myself sitting on that plane, surrounded by strangers, sobbing, accepting the tissues that they were offering me, shocked, and completely devastated.

"Cherie, are you sitting down? Are you around other people right now?"

"Well, yes, I'm still on the plane. Why? What happened?"

"Cherie, Clark committed suicide over Spring Break. The funeral was yesterday. We stayed back to wait for you and be here for you when you got home."

It had been only two weeks since I had seen him and heard his voice last. It had been two short weeks since he had said "goodbye" and wished me a great time on my trip. It had only been a few months since we had sat together and shared with each other all that was going on in our lives. We had both been through some difficult things that year, but hadn't everybody? We were seniors in college who carried the weight of midterms and finals on our shoulders. We all looked toward graduation day with mixed emotions, unsure of what our futures would hold. We all had experienced heartache and loss to some degree. Why Clark?

As the grief set in, so did the questions. How could this have happened? Why did he believe that there was no other way? Where was God in this? Will the pain ever go away? Not that suicide ever makes sense, but Clark seemed to be the least likely candidate. He was smart and accomplished. He was a leader on campus. He loved God. We just never truly saw the depth of his inner pain. Despite the fact that our lives overlapped so much, his struggle was hidden well. We had served together in student leadership. We had spent hours talking about school, God, relationships, and life after college. He had been such a good friend to me. As I received this news over the phone, four years of memories came rushing to my mind in this one, devastating moment. How could I have missed his pain? How did I not see it? How could he possibly be gone?

A dark cloud descended on my heart in that moment, and for what felt like years, I stumbled through those last few months at school in a haze. Tears felt like my companion. I cried so much that I felt there were no tears left to cry. Sorrow gripped me like I had never known. So many questions filled my mind, questions I had never found myself asking before. Hopelessness clouded my days.

I remained a leader on campus. I did graduate with honors. I held the love of that boy, for a time, however, that also found a way out of my life. I was left with what felt like little more than my despair. At the end of my first summer post college, hope was no longer on my horizon. Perhaps it had jumped ship to someone else's. My heart was heavy, and every day hurt. All that I had put my hope in had vanished. No dream job. No boy. No future. No hope.

But wait.

What is hope?

A definition of hope that I had yet to even uncover began to make its way into my life. There were days when I pleaded with God to take me home. There were days when I heard Him speak to me and ask, "Is that really what you want, Cherie? Because I am able to do that, right here, right now. Is that really what you want?" His firm but gentle response was all I needed to slowly wake me from my slumber, wake me from my grief.

As I began to listen more to Him, I found myself listening less to my hurt, less to my damaged emotions, less to the ache within me. I found myself running to His Word as the source for my comfort and less to my bed to escape the pain that tormented me. I began to learn that my hope, too, had been misplaced. I had wrongly placed my hope in things and people, when all along, Jesus was inviting me to place my hope in Him. As I journeyed down this new road, a path I had infrequently walked before, I found that Jesus can in fact turn my mourning into dancing. He can in fact bring beauty from the ashes. He can in fact deposit hope into the hopeless heart. Because I found that Jesus is hope. To find Him is to know hope. This hope is our firm foundation.

Hope is a strong and confident expectation. Hope is unwavering trust in the unchanging character of God.

> You turned my wailing into dancing;
>   you removed my sackcloth and
>   clothed me with joy,
>
> Psalm 30:11

and provide for those who grieve in
   Zion—
to bestow on them a crown of beauty
   instead of ashes,
the oil of joy
   instead of mourning,
and a garment of praise
   instead of a spirit of despair.

Isaiah 61:3

CHAPTER 2

HOPE BELIEVES

WHAT DOES BELIEF look like to you? How is it fleshed out? What does unwavering trust lived out in the day to day of our lives actually look like? Can you grasp an understanding of it? Can you even fathom it? In what do we really, truly believe anymore, anyway?

Hope believes the promises of God. Hope depends upon them. Hope knows that God can be taken at His Word. There is simply no other way to maintain hope than to understand that it is intrinsically connected to trust and faith. Our capacity to trust God and to have faith in His promises for us will directly impact our ability to possess and maintain hope in our lives. Likewise, our hope in the Lord will deeply impact our trust and faith in Him.

Do you see the connection?

For as long as I can remember, I've absolutely loved the 23rd Psalm. By the age of 10, I'd heard it more times than I could count, and I had memorized its six short verses. Blame it on Christian school or being in church nearly every single day of the week, but as I look back on those early years of my life, I'm increasingly grateful for those who helped lay my foundation of faith and invested in teaching me Scripture at such a young age.

Knowledge retention is much stronger and more effective when we are young. We can far more easily remember the things we memorized when we were young than the things we learned yesterday. Anybody else find this to be true? When I was in fourth grade, I learned all of the Presidents of the United States from beginning to end in order to the tune of a song. I'm telling you with all honesty that I can still sing that song to you today without skipping a beat or a name, but what I find to be so hilarious is that I have a much harder time remembering the most recent Presidents in order.

The same principle applies with all of the Bible verses I have memorized throughout my life. Psalm 23 was one chapter of Scripture that I learned at a young age, and I still know it well to this day. I could recite it for you at the drop of a hat. However, verses from the book of James or Ephesians that I've been trying to commit to memory over these past few years … well, let's just say that those are still a work in progress.

The verses that I memorized when I was a child have not only stuck with me, but I've seen how they have shaped my understanding of who God is, how He works, and His promises to me. I'll be the first to admit that I had my own season of wandering away from the Lord. Who hasn't, right? I didn't always walk faithfully with Jesus, and there are times when I still don't. However, there are certain truths from which I simply never departed, and certain promises found in the Word of God that I always believed to be true. Therefore, there was a certain level of hope which I always possessed, even when the fiercest storms raged in my heart.

Because hope believes the promises of God.

Psalm 23 is filled with promises. I don't know if you knew that or not, but it is. My first understanding of the 23rd Psalm was not much more than the fact that is was a portion of Scripture that was often read at funerals or included in the program. It wasn't until I was in my 20s that I began to really dig into God's Word, but before that time in my life, my understanding of Scripture was only surface deep. I would connect certain passages to experiences I had, or I would understand other parts through the lens of my own circumstances. Knowledge and understanding come through deeper study. So, I began to dig, and before I knew it, the rich promises of God were beginning to be found and realized in my own life.

I can remember being amazed when I realized that this chapter of Scripture wasn't one about death, but rather, these six verses breathe life from their words. There's a particular verse in the 23rd Psalm that explains why I would most often be exposed to it at funerals and memorial services. You're probably familiar with it, too.

> *Even though I walk through the valley of*
> *the shadow of death,*
> *I will fear no evil,*
> *for you are with me;*
> *your rod and your staff,*
> *they comfort me.*

Psalm 23:4 ESV

The valley of the shadow of death has a certain ring to it—an appropriate tune when grieving the loss of life. It was not until a few years ago, after going through a study of Psalm 23, that I learned what this phrase was referring to: the valley of deep darkness. Could this be referring to literal death? Sure, of course it could, but there's something about this wording that opens up the conversation for so much more.

Welcome to the conversation of this chapter: Hope Believes. As we take a deeper look at this Psalm, we will find six promises of God that are illuminated within. My prayer for each of us as we read and study is that these promises will awaken hope within us. As we choose to believe that these promises are for us, may hope stir within us in ways like never before, because hope stir within us in ways like never before, because hope believes the promises of God.

The promise of contentment

It's hard to imagine living a life that knows no lack. I'm not sure I've ever truly been in a place in my life when I had no wants and was truly content. Discontentment plagues us, and the desire for more strangles out the joy for that which we already have. It's ironic really, because we live with so much excess that we're nearly choking on it. We fill our homes with stuff, and the extra floods into our garages. What doesn't fit there goes into storage, and still we keep accumulating more.

The next best thing quickly overshadows what we already have, and we find ourselves lacking contentment even in our abundance. What if there was a better way? What if we didn't live life holding our breath for something better, and instead realized that the best has already been given to us?

> *The Lord is my shepherd; I shall not want.*
>
> Psalm 23:1

Here's the thing. When we choose to make the Lord the shepherd of our lives, we want not. See how that works?

We choose to want from Him, and all our wants are met in Him. When we choose to raise our empty cups to Him first, He fills them. The promise of contentment awaits. Hope believes.

The promise of rest

I find it equally hard to imagine being fully rested. If there are any moms of littles in the trenches with me today, you know full well what I'm saying. Life without little children can be equally exhausting. We are busy and tasked from sun up to sun down, and rest often escapes us in the frantic frenzy of trying to get everything done. What if there was a better way?

God's Word actually promises us that there is, in fact, a better way. Once again, it involves believing that the promises of God are true. Rest, true rest that far surpasses what sleep itself could provide, is found in the Lord when we choose to make Him our shepherd.

> *He makes me lie down in green*
> *pastures.*
> *He leads me beside still waters.*
> *He restores my soul.*
>
> Psalm 23:2-3a

Did you notice the imperatives in this verse? The phrases

"He makes" and "He leads" have strong implications. In essence, this one verse promises that God will ensure that we find rest if we have made Him the shepherd of our lives. He will make us lie down. He will lead us beside waters that are still—waters that will provide a stillness for our souls. This rest can be found in Him and Him alone. It's a rest for our very souls.

A rest like this can only be found in places of hope: a strong and confident expectation, an unwavering trust in the unchanging character of God. Why? Rest knows that in the absence of my own efforts, God remains in control. Rest believes that if we cease striving, the world will keep on spinning, and the God of the Universe will not be moved. Rest awaits those who believe His promise to be true. The promise of rest awaits you. Hope believes.

The promise of guidance

The question I am about to ask is one that I already know the answer to. If we were in the same room, I would receive a resounding "yes" as the answer, but I think this next promise still begs that the question be asked. So, here goes. Have you ever been at a crossroads in your life, desperate to know which direction you should go, but unable to move in any direction at all because you need guidance? That's what I thought. Me, too.

These can be the most challenging times in our faith, especially when both roads seem to be good ones. How do we choose between two great things? How do we choose between two difficult things? There's a promise for that.

> *He leads me in paths of righteousness*
> *for his name's sake.*
>
> Psalm 23:3b

The promise of God's guidance and direction is ours for the taking when we assume the position of follower. When we make the Lord the shepherd of our lives, He promises that He will guide us down "right paths." Notice the tagline to this promise: "for His name's sake." In other words, He will do this for His glory, for the fame of His own name. Did you know that God cares far more about His own glory than you or I ever could? It's true. While we exist to bring Him glory, we constantly fall short of that calling. Because God is God and we are not, He ensures that glory will be brought to His name. Don't you just love how He does that? He ensures His own glory by fulfilling promises to us. He will guide us. He will lead us. We must simply follow. The promise of His guidance awaits you. Hope believes.

The promise of protection

The battle of the hopeless is one that is so often defined by loneliness. When those valleys of deep darkness come knocking on our doors, feelings of isolation seem to accompany the darkness. It's hard to see in the dark, so we often assume that no one is there, and that this struggle is somehow unique to our own experience. Comfort and solace escape us, and we begin to doubt in the dark what we always knew to be true in the light.

God has a rich promise to deposit into the heart who feels hopeless today in the darkness—the promise of His protection in the midst of the darkness. Don't allow yourself to miss this critical point in verse four: The valleys of deep darkness will come. It's not a question of if they will come, but rather it is a question of when they will come. These dark valleys will look different in your life than they will look in mine, but we know that they will come. So, the psalmist writes,

> *Even though I walk through the valley of the shadow of death, I will fear no evil, for you are with me; your rod and your staff, they comfort me."*
>
> *Psalm 23:4*

As certain as the psalmist is that these deep, dark valleys will come, he is just as certain that God will be present with him in it, providing His protection. We simply cannot be unprotected when the presence of God is with us. If nothing else, when we have the constant presence of Jesus Christ by our side in the valley, our hearts are protected from the destructive and damaging emotions that darkness seeks to bring with it.

Can you hear this promise calling out to you today? The promise of God's protection over you in the darkness of your valley is made available to you. When we make the Lord the shepherd of our lives, we know the promise of His protection. It awaits you today. Hope believes.

The promise of provision

I love the names of God throughout Scripture. It is through the reading of God's Word that we learn of His character and of who He says He is. One of my favorite attributes of God is that He is Provider: Jehovah Jirah, the Lord my Provider. This one name of God is packed full of promise. God provides for His children. We can know this to be true of Him, and Psalm 23 is just one of many places throughout Scripture that points toward this truth.

> *You prepare a table before me in the presence of my enemies; you anoint my head with oil; my cup overflows.*
>
> *Psalm 23:5*

Have you ever felt like your enemies are triumphing over you? Can you relate to the many Psalms that speak to this struggle? Here you are doing good, walking faithfully with God, choosing right, and there are your enemies over there, getting away with murder, thriving in their wrongdoing. It seems so unfair, doesn't it?

Say hello to our next promise. God provides, and even in the very presence of our enemies, He will make known His provision for those who choose to make the Lord their shepherd. Hope believes that this promise is true. Hope believes that one day God will set all things right because He is a good, faithful, and just God. When the world has beaten us down and our cups have run dry, God will pour Himself into us until we overflow.

That is the abundant life. This is the promise of God for you. He will provide for your needs. He will make all things right. He will bring overflow to the places in our hearts that have become a dry, desert-like land. The promise of His provision awaits. Hope believes.

The promise of favor

Words hold a special place in my heart. I love words. I love the meaning of words. I love learning new words. The word favor is one with which I'm familiar, but it's a word that holds a depth of meaning of which I wasn't fully aware until recently. Favor means excessive kindness and unfair partiality. Doesn't that just take this conversation to a whole new level?

The promise of God's favor rests upon us as His children when we choose to make Him our shepherd. I love that. God's excessive kindness and unfair partiality is promised to us when we choose to make the Lord our shepherd. Don't just take my word for it. Take His Word for it.

> *Surely goodness and mercy shall follow me all the days of my life, and I shall dwell in the house of the Lord forever.*
>
> *Psalm 23:6*

I don't know how this one verse contains so much promise, but it does. The verse begins with the word "surely." In other translations, that word could be "only." So, "only goodness and mercy" will be following after me every day of my life. Can you even imagine? This is what the favor of the Lord looks like, and I want an extra measure of it. Don't you? I want to know this kind of blessing in my life—blessing that far exceeds material possessions, status, fame, or anything else that this world promises will make us happy. I want joy! I want the everlasting!

The promise of God's favor is for you, and it is for me. It

awaits us. Hope believes that these and so many more promises are true. I have tasted the fulfillment of these promises in my own life, and so has Jessica.

This is her hope story.

Jessica's journey with God in some ways has paralleled my journey with the study of Scripture. She was young when she was first introduced to Jesus, and faith began to grow within her heart. It wasn't until her junior year in high school, though, when she began to really embrace and understand the promises of God for her. All that she had learned about God as a child was developing into so much more. These truths were taking deeper root in her life, and she was running full steam ahead with her newfound faith in Jesus.

Transferring to a Christian school only added to her thrill because she was now surrounded by a rich environment of faith. She was learning more about the Bible, more about Jesus, and more about what it looked like to really follow Him, and she was loving every minute of it. She couldn't get enough of God's Word. She would read it, journal about it, and post verses and truth from Scripture all over the walls of her room. The landscape of her life was beginning to be completely covered with Jesus.

As she continued to grow in her faith, the soil of her life was rich for receiving the truth. The more she learned, the more she believed. The more promises she uncovered, the more hope filled her heart. Little did she know that this season of thirst for the Word of God would be what carried her through the storms that were about to come.

When she met the boy, she was in such a good place. She was trusting God, and she thought he was, too. Love is a powerful emotion, though, and over the course of time, her love for this boy began to overshadow her love for God. His voice became the loudest voice in her life—louder than the voice of God and His Word. She didn't realize at the time that this was happening because her emotions had clouded her vision—vision that had once been so clear.

The more he pressured her, the more she gave in. She loved him. He promised her things, too. He promised love. He promised marriage. He promised a good life together. So, she kept giving more and more of herself to him. She loved him. When they had sex for the first time, the promise given to her then was that they were going to be married someday anyway, so it was ok. He had become her everything. She was tied to him, and she was no longer sure where she ended and he began.

What started with pressure quickly turned into control. He began to control her and every part of her life. The control then quickly turned to abuse. He would scare her into submission. She didn't want to stay, but she was so afraid to leave. Her fear caused her to fall into a deep depression. She knew she needed to get away because it was getting increasingly dangerous for her to stay.

In a rush of fear, coupled with moments of certainty and confidence, and too ashamed and afraid to go home to her parents, she packed her bags, left him, and went to her aunt's house—a place of refuge and a trusted source of love and truth in her life. She knew she had made the right decision in leaving, but she also knew that she needed help to carry out this decision to completion. She couldn't do it alone.

The threats came, and the fear remained, but she refused to waver in her decision. She was not going back. She would wait it out if she had to, but she would never return to that life of control and abuse. Her aunt had always been a voice of comfort and hope in her life, and being in her presence was restoring some hope back into Jessica's heart, as they waited this nightmare out together.

He eventually stopped calling, and the threats eventually ended as well, but her depression only darkened. Alcohol was the first substance that was sought to numb the pain, but it never could fully accomplish what she desired it to. The walls were high and deeply fortified around her heart. She wasn't interested in letting anyone in, but she was willing to entertain the idea of having a little fun. Perhaps the fun would numb the pain that alcohol couldn't.

Poor choices in men continued. It wasn't about love. It was the pursuit of pleasure, but that pursuit kept coming up empty. It wasn't long before she dropped out of college, and all the hope that she had once possessed seemed like nothing more than a distant memory. Now medicated for her depression and seeing a counselor, she was desperate for relief from this pain, trying everything to find it—everything but Jesus.

It's amazing how God shows up, even when we aren't looking for Him, and we're no where near ready to follow Him. In the midst of this darkness and hopelessness, she met a few girls who encouraged her to go back to school and to run track with them. Even though they were playing the same games that she was, she now had something to look forward to. She had something to live for. Glimmers of hope were beginning to find their way back into her life. God was trying to get her attention again, trying to remind her that He had created her on purpose and with a purpose.

Still terrified at the thought of another relationship but willing to entertain the idea of casual dating, she continued to find herself giving more pieces of herself away to one boy after the other. Free from consequences and the fear of getting hurt once again, she thought she had it all figured out. So, when she met the next guy, she was relieved to know that he wanted nothing more than fun, as well.

Their season of fun ended rather abruptly when she found out that she was pregnant. She was 20 years old and had her entire life ahead of her. She had dreams for her future. She had hopes and plans, but they all seemed to come to a screeching halt when that test came back positive. She hit rock bottom. Even in the deepest, darkest parts of her depression, she had never been this low. Mixed reactions from friends and family in response to the news of her pregnancy turned her heart back to God and His voice. She needed a constant once again. She had no one else to turn to but Him. She had no where else to look but up.

There is something about hitting rock bottom that almost forces us to look up. There is something about brokenness that causes us to look to the Healer. She found herself seeking God through prayer for the first time in years, once again finding hope resurfacing in her heart. She immediately felt His presence, guidance, and covering in the time of greatest uncertainty in her life. What had begun as shame was beginning to be replaced with newfound hope. She knew He had forgiven her.

All of the promises of God she had learned in high school

began to resurface in her mind, and she knew that all she had to do was turn back to Him. These promises could be realized in her life once again. Why had she chosen to turn to all these other things when God and His love for her was what she had always been looking for?

God was holding her hand through the pregnancy and all of the unknowns. Would they get married? Would she be a single mom? How would she afford to raise a child? What would life look like now? Even in the midst of all her questions and uncertainty, she had hope. It wasn't easy, and it certainly wasn't painless, but she learned once again that what could be a hopeless situation is never hopeless with God. She knew she was going to be ok.

Becoming a mom brought her back into the arms of Jesus. Although she knows now that He had never left her side, she had certainly tried to run from Him. The challenges that awaited her would have overwhelmed her if she had seen them coming all at once, but God faithfully and consistently led her through each one—being a single mom, learning a new way of life, finding faith once again, returning to godly community at a great church, and meeting and falling in love with her future forever.

She now has ten years of marriage behind her and three more beautiful children, and this road hasn't been easy either. It's been good, though. It's been refining and stretching every step of the way. It's been both hard and delightful. On every mountain top and in every valley, she has learned to rehearse the promises of God. She has learned once again to believe His promises are for her. She has learned to hope in them because it has been God's love for her alone that has rescued her, and she will be forever grateful for the story He has written for her. It's not finished yet, but hope remains and hope believes the promises along the way.

CHAPTER 3

HOPE REMEMBERS

THERE IS SOMETHING so real about mourning. It's an incredibly tangible emotion that can leave us grasping at straws to find our footing amidst seasons of grief. Mourning gives voice to our pain. Mourning reveals our humanness when we so often try to hide it. There is an authenticity and vulnerability that accompanies mourning that has the ability to awaken something inside of us that we, perhaps, didn't realize had fallen into slumber.

Hope.

Like you, I am all too aware of the taste of mourning. Waves of grief have threatened to swallow me whole in my own times of loss and heartache, and had it not been for the hope of Jesus, I wouldn't be writing these words today. I wouldn't know them to be true. When I actually take the time to think about it, I don't know how anyone gets through this life without this hope. How does one face the difficulty of today and the unknowns of tomorrow without this strong and confident expectation, this unwavering trust in the unchanging character of God?

I'm here to tell you today that hope is real. Hope is alive, and I have found that the only way to survive the devastation that life so often brings is to remember how faithful God has been in our past. Hope does many things, but one thing it does is remember. Hope remembers who God was in the past. Hope rehearses what He has already done. This remembering brings with it a knowing that because He was faithful then, God will remain faithful now.

It is too easy to lose sight of that knowledge when we find ourselves in the middle of deep pain; but if we are ever going to know hope, it is critical that we choose to remember. If we could lift our eyes from the ashes around us for long enough to look back on how God has so faithfully carried us through the past painful trials of our lives, I am confident that we would regain some supernatural vision for our present pain and for the unknown of our future. Hope remembers God's faithfulness.

The prophet Jeremiah was also no stranger to devastating loss. He knew it all too well. He walked hand in hand with brokenness, pain, and heartache. In fact, he was so well acquainted with loss and tragedy that he became known as "The weeping prophet." How's that for a title? Forgive me, but I'd much prefer "the beloved disciple" or "a man (in my case, woman) after God's own heart."

Nevertheless, Jeremiah had a reputation for weeping, but he also had good reason for it. The book of Lamentations records his lament over the state of Judah. The temple of God had been destroyed, and the people of God had been taken into captivity. As Jeremiah stumbled through the destruction and remains of Jerusalem, his grieving and mourning poured out onto the pages of what we now hold in our hands as the book of Lamentations. It is a cry of grief that lasts five chapters, but tucked right in the middle of this lengthy lament are some of the most hope-filled words in all of Scripture.

> *Yet this I call to mind and therefore I have hope.*
>
> Lamentations 3:21

Before we take one step further into what exactly Jeremiah called to mind, let us not miss the fact that he called to mind. In just a few words, he exemplifies something incredibly profound to us all. He chooses to remember. He had just spent over three chapters of Scripture mourning and grieving, but he chooses to pause long enough to remember that God had been ever so faithful to His people in the past. Did you notice the result of his choice?

Hope.

In the middle of devastation, Jeremiah is able to regain hope, that is hard for us to fully understand, by simply choosing to remember the faithfulness of God. This is huge, and we need to grasp something from this one short verse in Scripture if you and I are ever going to be hope-filled in this hard life. We, too, must choose to call to mind. We must choose to remember. Hope chooses to remember.

What did Jeremiah choose to remember? Well, this is where it gets really good. Let's take a look together at the next few verses of Lamentations 3, and as we do, let us choose to know and believe that these words of promise are just as much for you and me today as they were for Jeremiah and God's people then.

> *Because of the Lord's great love we are not consumed, for his compassions never fail.*
>
> Lamentations 3:22

I am obsessed with this verse, absolutely obsessed. I can't tell you how many times I forget its truth, but hope floods my heart, just as it did Jeremiah's, when I remember its presence in Scripture. I have felt consumed by painful circumstances more times than I can count, and I know you have, as well. Life is painful. We know it is good, too, but that knowledge doesn't always lessen the blow of the painful times, does it? Life is hard, but hope comes rushing in when we remember who God says He is in His Word.

In just this one verse alone, we are given more reason to possess and maintain hope than we could ever need. The Lord's love for us is so great that not even the most fiery trial could consume us. Not even the deepest waters could overwhelm us. Not even the lowest valleys or the darkest darkness could destroy us. His compassions (or in some versions, His mercies) never, ever fail. Those two truths allow hope to soar, but we have to remember them. We have to call them to mind. We must choose.

Think back to your most recent hardship, a difficulty in which you now find yourself on the other side. In looking back and in seeing that you have been brought through, although not necessarily without a scar or two along the way, can you see a bit more clearly in hindsight the faithfulness of God? Can you detect His presence in your pain? Hope looks back to remember. Hope remembers His faithfulness. Hope knows the promises of God's great love and His unfailing mercies.

*They are new every morning; great is
your faithfulness.*

Lamentations 3:23

If the first two promises were not enough, God, in His
great love, follows them with this assurance. Do you
remember that great love and compassion that we just
read about in the last verse? Do you remember those
mercies that never fail? Well, add to that the truth that we
are met with His mercy anew each and every morning,
and exhale a huge sigh of relief. Was yesterday an epic
fail? His mercies are new toward you this morning!
Did you mess up so much this past week that you no
longer feel worthy of His forgiveness? His mercies are
new toward you today! Is the weight of the trial you are
enduring more than you can shoulder? His mercies
come rushing to meet you afresh this morning! That is
how faithful our God is.

Can we just stop and revel in the goodness of that
promise for a moment? It's worth an extra minute of our
time. His mercy never runs out even when we do. His
mercy outruns our rebellion. His mercy is stronger than
our burden. His mercy provides a clean slate for each
new day that we face. His mercy wakes us every morning
with fresh breath in our lungs and a renewed sense of
hope for our souls. His mercy cannot be outmatched. His
mercy never fails.

This ought to change something inside of us. It ought to awaken desire within us. If all of this is true, then what other response can we have but hope? How else could we respond to that kind of love, that amount of compassion, and that endless supply of mercy? Jeremiah knew no other way to respond than the words he penned in verse 24.

> *I say to myself, "The Lord is my portion;*
> *therefore I will wait for him.*
>
> Lamentations 3:24

No other words better portray a strong and confident expectation, and an unwavering trust in the unchanging character of God than those words do. Jeremiah had chosen to make God his portion—a determined choice to have all of his very real needs met in the Lord. He chose to wait on the Lord in His grief, and the very real and known result was hope. Jeremiah knew hope in what was the most hopeless circumstance of His life. Why? Jeremiah knew that hope wasn't found in desirable circumstances. Rather, hope is found in the One who controls those circumstances.

These can be incredibly difficult words to reconcile when we find ourselves in undesirable places. If God is good and faithful, and we simultaneously find ourselves in devastating places, how do we reconcile what we see, feel, and experience with a God whom we can't see? Some of the most difficult questions in this life pale in comparison to this one: How can God be good when everything around me isn't?

Jeremiah wasn't the only one to walk painful paths and still come to this knowledge of hope in the midst of his pain. Countless faithful followers of the Lord have experienced pain that seems so undeserving, so unfair, so hard, and so cruel. Just take a look at Hebrews 11. We could reflect on those who have been martyred for their faith. We could think of every widow and orphan in their distress. We could question the goodness of God in the face of cancer and suicide and addiction. Still, there are those who have been found faithful in the midst of hopeless circumstances like these, and there has been one common denominator that has linked their pain to their faithfulness.

Hope remembers God's faithfulness.

I am not suggesting to you that it is easy. It's not. It might be the hardest thing you ever do in this life, but it is possible, and it is worth every ounce of effort put forth. Choosing to rehearse God's faithfulness does not remove your right to grieve and to mourn the loss and the pain. Please hear this and know beyond a shadow of a doubt: Jeremiah was warranted an entire book of the Bible to weep. Cry every tear, my friend. Weep and mourn and grieve your losses. Jesus did, and so should we. We must grieve and mourn the pain, but we must not get stuck there. In Christ, there is life after death. In Christ, there is hope after despair. In Christ, there is healing after suffering. In Christ, there is abundance after lack. In Christ, there is beauty after ashes. So, allow sorrow to last for the night of your pain, but know that joy comes in the morning, along with His new mercies. It's who He is.

If you and I are ever going to be named among the faithful cloud of witnesses that have gone before us, then we need to determine for ourselves today that we will do the same. We must choose to look back, not for the sake of dwelling on the pain, but rather for the purpose of remembering His faithfulness in the pain. We must choose to see how present He has been in our hurt, and we must choose to believe that His presence then gives us hope in His presence now. We must choose to remember. We must determine whose voice will be loudest in our lives. Will it be the voice of our pain or the voice of our Healer? We can choose to remember. I can choose to remember. You can choose to remember. Lindsay chose to remember.

This is her hope story.

From as early as she could remember, Lindsay had always desired to get married. She was easily able to picture herself as the beautiful bride, but there was an apprehension surrounding the thought of becoming a mother one day. I'm sure somewhere inside of her, she wanted to be a mom, but the desire wasn't quite as natural.

Everything changed the day that Mark walked into her life. There is something about knowing the one with whom you will spend your future that makes the unknown of that future a bit less daunting. She knew that he would be an incredible dad some day, and as they grew together, her fears and apprehension began to fade. Desire, anticipation, and even hope for motherhood now replaced the feelings that once had taken up residence in her heart. God had been so good and so faithful to not only bring her a godly husband, but He also surrounded her with a community of friends who modeled such great parenting. Slowly but surely, she was beginning to feel more and more equipped to enter into that stage of life with Mark by her side.

Having walked with the Lord for much of her life, it was not difficult for Lindsay to detect when God was trying to get her attention about something. If she found herself within a season of what seemed to be constant teaching from the Lord, that particular message would come regularly and from all directions, even unexpected ones. It's easy for her now to look back over the course of her life and see this pattern of God's pursuit of her heart, but when in the middle of it, it can be so challenging to understand the message He is trying to send.

A few years into their marriage, Lindsay repeatedly found herself in Matthew 13 and the parable of the sower. The same seed fell on four different types of soil: the path, the rocky ground, the thorns, and the good soil. Naturally, the seed responded differently in each environment. It was trampled under foot on the path. It was scorched by the sun and withered on the rocky ground because there wasn't adequate soil for the seed to take root. It was choked out by the thorns. The seed only grew and flourished on the good soil.

It seemed that wherever she went, whatever she read, whoever she listened to preach, and whichever station was on the radio, this message of the sower and the seed kept popping up. A song, a message at church, a text from a friend, homework from her Bible study, and countless other voices kept speaking this same message, this same Jesus story into her life. "God, I get you're trying to get my attention with this, but why?"

Not knowing the answer to her own question, she was still determined to learn and to grow. She wanted to be the good soil that received the seed, the soil that allowed the seed to grow. She recognized the warning about the hard, rocky soil, and found herself praying often to not be found in that place—unable to receive what the Lord wanted to give. If nothing else, she knew He was impressing these imperatives on her heart: Cling to Jesus. Cling to His Word. Cling to hope. "God, when your truth comes, help me to readily receive it and for it to take root in my heart." Little did she know, but God was already at work preparing the soil of her heart, in ways that only He can, for the season of life that was about to come.

You're never quite prepared to receive the news of pregnancy, and it certainly comes with mixed emotions. There is often shock coupled with thrill that is laced with bits of fear, and it seems to cycle through those and other emotions for some time before the reality of it all sets in. Then the excitement comes, and it lingers. Their news came rather quickly once they had decided to try to start a family. A positive pregnancy test led to two short weeks of joy and anticipation, but the rush of it all came to a screeching halt one Sunday morning when I received a call from a frightened and very worried Lindsay. "Cherie, I think I'm having a miscarriage."

Losing a child, at any age and under any circumstance, is a pain like none other. She was devastated. The ache of her loss was palpable. Her tears were her companion, but even in the times of her deepest grief and sorrow, she could sense the sweet kindness of the Lord toward her. "Don't forget me in this, Lindsay. Don't forget truth and hope." In the immediate aftermath of this devastating loss, the message of Matthew 13 came rushing to her eyes and ears yet again. "Be the good soil. Refuse to be hardened by this pain. Receive the seed of my truth, and allow it to flourish and grow into something so beautiful."

So, she did. Although not perfectly, she began to take small steps every day in the same direction back into the arms of her Savior, and it was this return journey that carried her through that storm. She decided to meet the Lord in the hurt. She chose to allow Him to take the ashes of her pain and make something beautiful from them.

When the news of pregnancy number two came just a few months later, she was nearly certain that this was how God was going to redeem the brokenness of the first loss. Every day that they made it past the length of her first pregnancy instilled more hope in her heart. It was music to their ears the first time they heard that sweet baby's heartbeat. Could it be that this would be the healing balm on her wounded heart for which she had so desperately longed?

Grief, sorrow, and loss do not discriminate. They are no respecter of persons, and absolutely nothing could have prepared them for what came next. "I'm so sorry to deliver this news, but there is no heartbeat." What had seemed like nine long weeks of a successful pregnancy had now ended, and their hearts were crushed once again.

"God, where are you? This is not fair. Did I not already pass your test with our first loss? Now, this? I can't walk this road again. Why do I have to? I don't want this to be my story."

As hard as the days and weeks were that followed their first loss, this seemed so much worse. How does one reconcile a good God with human suffering? She knew the truth about God and His character, in theory. She had a Bible college degree. She was a worship leader. She was a Christian music artist. Her whole life was about pointing people to the love of Jesus Christ, but in these uncharted waters of pain, she wasn't sure how to transfer the knowledge of God's love for her from her head down to her heart.

That shift from a knowledge of God to a love for God can take some time, but I have found that it most readily occurs in the seasons of our hurt, heartache, and loss. It's as if the soil of our hearts is somewhat ripened for growth through the brokenness. When we find ourselves on the floor of the pit of our pain, there is no where else for us to look but up. It took time for the truth that the Lord truly loved her, and that He was going to see her through this, to sink in, but in the pain of devastating loss, she came to believe that these promises of God were actually for her, too, and not just everyone else.

I remain confident of this: I will see the

goodness of the Lord in the land of the living.

Psalm 27:13

The Lord is close to the brokenhearted and saves those who are crushed in spirit.

Psalm 34:18

Lindsay had to learn that it was one thing to believe in God, but it was quite another to believe God—to truly take Him at His Word. These rich promises, among others, began to come to life within her for the first time, bringing new life to places long devastated. The God whom she had spoken so confidently of, from platforms around the world, was now becoming a personal, loving, faithful, and good Father to her wounded heart.

Brokenhearted people don't often tend to think that the Lord is near to them. They think that He's far, that He's forgotten them, and that He's gone. The Lord loves us so much, though, and so He put the promise of Psalm 34:18 in His Word to remind us that nothing is wasted in His presence. Pain is a holy experience, because that is where His presence meets us. It is in our pain that the nearness of His presence becomes so tangible. It was in her pain that she found this to be true.

This was the hope that she clung to in her brokenness. Her surroundings all but screamed that God had abandoned her, but God's Word spoke a better word over her. In the midst of her pain and her struggle to navigate the waves of grief, she was scrolling through Facebook one day and came across this description of miscarriages: "God's abortions." It broke her heart realizing that people could see it that way. One glimpse of that lie awakened her to truth. While God may have allowed it, He did not do it. God's heart is life for us. Our hope is alive because our hope is Jesus.

Throughout the early years of her marriage and certainly through this season of ache and loss, the Lord had consistently been drawing her attention to this: Come into God's presence with thanksgiving. She had led countless others in worship with this invitation, and the Lord had been gently wooing her with the same invitation. Why does the Lord desire for us to do that? Well, first and foremost, He's flat out worthy of our praise, but it doesn't stop there. He loves us and He knows that when we recall to mind His faithfulness—all of the reasons in our past that we have to thank God—it stirs a holy confidence within us to believe that He will be faithful in our future.

One night shortly after the first miscarriage, the tears were streaming down her face as she held tightly to

Mark, feelings of anger, sadness, and deep hurt raging within her heart. In a moment she will never forget, these thoughts of truth began to speak just a little louder than her pain: "What about Jesus? Don't you remember Jesus? Did He not also feel the pain of devastating loss?"

She wept again, tears that came from a different place inside of her, because she remembered Jesus' love for her. Just the thought of His name brought her mind back to hope. He had always been there, even in her darkest night and deepest pain, and even though she couldn't see how He was doing it in that moment, He was going to make something beautiful out of this. That's just who He is, always working all things out for the good of those who love Him. So, how could she doubt His love for her now?

A new reality began to emerge from the ashes of her pain. She could see so much more clearly now why God tells us to give thanks in all circumstances. It doesn't mean we have to manufacture happiness in our broken seasons, but it is choosing to remember all the reasons why we can have joy. Whatever the situation that has changed in our lives, undesirable as it may be, it hasn't changed God. Knowing these truths began to allow hope to flourish within her once again.

The worry that was birthed in her through those first two

losses is a battle she is forced to overcome every day. Every time worry and fear try to rear their ugly heads, she puts her stake in the ground of her trial and chooses to remember. She knows well now that to rehearse God's faithfulness will breed faith and hope in her. With a confidence that she might not have known without the journey through the pain, she would tell you today that knowing Jesus has made it worth it all.

The Lord has been so good, and His promise to restore the years that the locusts have eaten (Joel 2:25) has been realized in her life. Malachi Lewis was welcomed into their world with great joy a year later. Delight and joy fill their days as they raise their son, knowing what a gift and an answer to their prayers he is.

Loss has marked many of the years of Lindsay's adult life. She and her family buried her beloved father just a few years before the loss of her two babes. A sudden and tragic loss of her brother-in-law followed soon after. In the wake of so much grief, many lessons have been learned along the way. First, and perhaps most importantly, she is committed and determined to refuse to allow the enemy to use this loss and pain for evil; instead, she has learned what it means to throw herself into the arms of God's faithfulness. She will remember His goodness. She will remember His presence in her pain. She will possess and maintain hope, because her hope is in Jesus.

Maybe the next greatest lesson learned is the eternal perspective that she now holds. You can be present in today and choose to recognize God's provision for you now, knowing that whatever may come, this hot pavement upon which we walk and stumble through our days is not our home. Remembering God's faithfulness toward us in our past only greater ensures a hope within us for the unknown of our future. Could it be that the horrors we face in this life, that we desperately wish we could have avoided, actually prove to be what sets our hearts ablaze for eternity?

Close your eyes and imagine the moment when you are finally in the presence of the Holy, reigning, ruler of the universe—that moment when you finally see God face to face. The longer we walk the ground of this painful world, the more our hearts are bent toward a longing for heaven, a place where there will be no more sin, no more sorrow, and no more death. How we handle loss and what we do with pain prepares us for our eternal home. Lindsay can now see the pain as a privilege that was entrusted to her because she learned how to cling to Jesus while she misses her babies. She can now enter His presence with thanksgiving because she learned what it means to be near to Him even more.

God is always using all things for good. We believe that He will because He always has. We choose to put our hope in Him and not in our circumstances. The choosing isn't in our strength; it's in His faithfulness. Because of His faithfulness, we can choose hope. By thanking Him and rehearsing what He's done, He sees us through the painful loss of today and the unknown losses of tomorrow. This hope is a holy confidence in the Lord's faithfulness.

Lindsay has the hope of eternity, knowing that her two sweet babies are alive and well with Jesus, and as one trusted friend shared with her, "Heaven gets more real when we have an investment there." Hope remembers God's faithfulness. Remember today with me, friends.

CHAPTER 4

HOPE EMBRACES

ADVERSITY IN LIFE is part of the human condition. I so wish it wasn't, but it is. Seasons of hardship and trials of many kinds are had and known by all people. If we are alive, we will experience this. It can not be avoided, despite our most valiant efforts. No one is immune to pain on this side of heaven. So, it's not a matter of if it will come, but rather, it's a matter of when it will come. What will we do with our pain when it arrives? How will we handle the hardship? Will we be hardened by it? Will we embrace it?

There is a truth that brings tremendous hope into the conversation of suffering, and it is this: There is purpose in our pain. To be a follower of Jesus Christ is to know and believe this to be true. Our pain is never in vain if we are in Christ because that is what His Word says. Faith is believing the Word of God. We get the choice to believe this truth and therefore live with hope, or we can deny this truth and continue searching for hope, meaning, and purpose in this hard life. If we take the latter route, our journey will be long and ultimately prove to be fruitless, ause hope is found in the One who created it.

To live in hope and to know hope in the face of unpleasant and unwanted circumstances is to have chosen to embrace those circumstances as part of God's greater, redemptive story for our lives. The writers of Scripture touched on this consistently throughout the Bible, and their hope-filled words have proven to deposit hope into weary souls time and time again. If we could just sit in these inspired words a bit longer than we dwell in our own uninspired thoughts, I imagine we would begin to see hope come alive within our suffering.

Let's go on a journey together through an age-old passage, and let's sit in the words of hope that are ours for the taking. Let's allow these words to ruminate in our minds and move into our hearts. Hope is not reserved for the elite or for those deemed worthy to receive it. Hope is for all. Hope is not distant or out of reach. Hope is not hard to find, if we are looking in the right place. Hope is meant to be our daily reality, a consciousness in which we live every moment. Hope is yours, and hope is mine. So, let's embrace hope for ourselves.

> *But now, this is what the Lord says—*
> *he who created you, Jacob,*
> *he who formed you, Israel:"*

Isaiah 43:1a

God, ever so graciously, reminds us of who He is before He tells us what we are to do. It's incredible, isn't it? A good, loving, and faithful God chose to make Himself known to us in order to build trust within us. He introduces Himself to us here with this one, beautiful description: He is our Creator, the One who formed us in our mother's womb. This one detail sheds so much light on the character of God. He is a God who gets involved with our lives. He gave great attention to the details of our form. He breathed life into our bones. He was intimately involved in the process. That shouts love. That invites relationship.

I love how God leans into our humanity with an introduction of who He is. It's an invitation, really—an invitation to know Him just as we are known by Him. It's an invitation to trust Him. The Creator of the sun, moon, and stars, the One who hung each one in their place in the sky, is the same One who fashioned you in His own image before human eyes ever saw your tiny frame. He is the One who has been there since the very beginning, and He is the One who holds together all things in the palm of His hand.

Knowing this attribute of God helps to lay a firm foundation upon which we can receive the next several verses in Isaiah 43. Scripture is about to get real in relation to our pain and suffering, and I for one wouldn't know how to embrace the promise of hardship in this life without knowing who God says He is first. He is the Creator of life; therefore, He is the sustainer of life. It rests in His hands, and in the heat of the fight to survive, God gives us some very precious promises, and He gives us words of hope to embrace in our storms.

> *Do not fear, for I have redeemed you;*
> *I have summoned you by name; you*
> *are mine."*
>
> Isaiah 43:1b

It amazes me how many times Scripture commands us not to fear. God knew we would be ever so prone to fear in the face of trying circumstances, so He chose to repeat Himself on this one, again and again. "Do not fear." That's not a suggestion. That's a command. Another thing I love about the Word of God is that every command is coupled with a promise. Take a look at it again. He commands us not to fear, and He immediately follows that command with a few reasons why obedience to that command is possible.

First, He has redeemed us. We don't need to wonder at that. If we are in Christ, redemption is already ours. Secondly, He knows your name. He knows mine. This is the beauty of relationship. We are not just a number to God. He knows our names. This is the beauty of friendship. Finally, He calls us His own. We are not abandoned. We are not orphaned. We are not alone. We are His. This is the beauty of belonging.

When we have all of this truth in place, we can read the words of Isaiah 43:2 with courage and hope instead of fear and despair. The waters are going to rise. We can be sure of it. The heat from the flame will oftentimes feel too hot and too close for comfort. We can count on it. However, by trusting in the character of God, we can embrace the journey. Hope embraces the process because hope knows that God is present in it.

> *When you pass through the waters,*
>   *I will be with you;*
> *and when you pass through the rivers,*
>   *they will not sweep over you.*
> *When you walk through the fire,*
>   *you will not be burned;*
>   *the flames will not set you ablaze."*

Isaiah 43:2

When the waters rise, God is there. When the rivers rage, God is there. When the fire blazes, God is there. When the hardship comes rolling in like the tide, you will not be swept away. Hope tethers us to an unwavering God. It anchors us. It renders us secure in His constant and careful hold.

I write these words of conviction, faith, and hope in the wake of devastating loss. My dear friend and her husband said goodbye to their 18-year-old son today. As we gathered together to celebrate his short life on this earth, the only thought that raced through my mind as the tears fell down my face was this: "This should not be." This was a life that had yet to fully live. This was a firstborn son. This is a heartache too deep and painful to understand. These are high waters and fierce flames, and I can only imagine how impossible this weight of grief must feel to those who loved him most. "This should not be."

I sat among hundreds who had come to love and support the family in their time of deepest sorrow. The grief in the room was all but tangible. You could taste it. You could feel it. You could see it. People held each other and wept in each other's arms. Tears openly flowed. It doesn't seem fair. The pain cuts too deep.

But God.

As the days, and now weeks, have unfolded since the devastating news of his passing, I've seen something else mingled with the grief. I've seen hope. In the face of what would be my worst nightmare, my courageous friend has daily chosen to trust the Lord in this fierce storm. It seems unfathomable to me, but there she remains, choosing to believe that God isn't finished yet.

She knows that this isn't the end of the story. She is confident that there is purpose in her pain. Every day, she resolves to believe that God remains good even when her circumstances aren't. She still weeps, but her hope embraces a God who is bigger than her battle.

Hope is not temporal. It is eternal. When we face trials of many kinds, we have a choice to make. We can either choose to run to God with our hurt, believing that the testing of our faith is intended to develop perseverance within us, or we can run away from God because of our hurt, falsely believing that a good God wouldn't allow such suffering. The former leads us to victory. The latter leads us to defeat.

I'm not suggesting to you that choosing to trust and believe that God is good is easy. I know it's not. I'm not assuming that your pain is small. I know it's not. I'm simply doing all that I know how to do when I face pain and loss in this life. I've tried running from God. That final destination proved to be not worth the journey. I've tried blaming God. That didn't work either. I've tried every negative response imaginable, and in my attempts to run from God, I've learned this truth:

God runs faster. He will outrun every single one of us every single time. We can't run from Him. We can try, but His love will keep chasing after us.

I've found it far more effective to run to Him with my pain, knowing that He remains the same even when my life does not. I've learned to believe that God is present in the rising waters that threaten to overwhelm me. I've learned that God protects me from the flames as they rage around me. I've learned what it means to hope.

Hope expects God to show up because He has been faithful to do so every single time in the past. Hope is confident in God's ability to overcome our greatest battle because He's seen us safely through the last one. Hope does not waver when the boat rocks back and forth on the raging seas because hope is tethered to an unwavering God.

How much time and energy do we waste in our doubt? How much hope is dashed in our lives because we will not take our eyes off of the seas to look into the face of the Savior? How much breakthrough awaits us if we would embrace what has been entrusted to us?

Times of sorrow have taught me to lift my eyes to the One who catches my tears. Times of fear have taught me to offer my heart to the One who can give me peace. Times of brokenness have taught me to surrender my pain to the One who can heal. He commands much, but dear friend, do not miss this: He promises so much more.

For I am the Lord your God,
    the Holy One of Israel, your Savior;
I give Egypt for your ransom,
    Cush and Seba in your stead.

Isaiah 43:3

The value that God places on us is worth more than nations. Don't miss that in verse three. He calls us worthy of rescue. He deems us worthy of His redemption. In His eyes, we were worth saving. In exchange for our lives, He gave His own. Hope chooses to embrace what may come because it knows that God's presence is a certainty in every storm we will weather.

Let me tell you two things of which I am confident. First, I am confident that I could not make it through tomorrow without the hope of Jesus. There is too much suffering and sorrow in this world to even want to try to make it through tomorrow without the hope of Christ. Actually, I have no idea how people do make it through without the hope of Christ. How does one face the loss of a child without the hope of Jesus? How does one face cancer without the hope of Christ? How does one live through the seemingly endless injustices in this world without the hope of Christ?

I don't know, but let me tell you the second thing of which I am confident. I am confident that I can make it through tomorrow because I have the hope of Jesus. There are countless unknowns that tomorrow will bring, but of this I am sure: Jesus is already there. He is already in my tomorrow, waiting for me to arrive. I can live with that. I can face what may come because I know that I am not going to face it alone. I can embrace every stop on my journey home because I can know that Jesus stops with me. I can run into the arms of God when I hurt because I know that He's waiting with arms open wide.

Hope isn't a theory, friends. Hope is a reality, and it can be known in your mess right now. The hope-filled heart embraces the journey because Jesus is ever present. He has been present in my mess, and He will be present in yours. I know this to be true, and so does Lori.

This is her hope story.

Lori was a fairly healthy child. Aside from the common cold and maybe some over the counter medications here and there, she was most often well. It wasn't until her high school years when it all began to change. The constant exhaustion set in first. She was always tired, but she didn't know why. Mom wasted no time in taking her to countless doctors' appointments, determined to find an answer, but no answers were ever given to explain why she felt the way she did. Tests were taken, but everything came back negative. It seemed the only answer they could give her was that perhaps she was too busy doing too many things.

Moving forward without any answers, she was left with only one choice. She learned how to live tired all the time. Years of exhaustion followed, and she slowly forgot what it felt like to be rested. Chronic fatigue was her new normal. She probably could have fared well with just the exhaustion, but intense and often excruciating pain joined the exhaustion a few years later. Crippling pain now seared through her body, and one day, she realized that she couldn't even use her hands. As she sat and stared down at her now crippled, bent, and swollen fingers, she knew something was terribly wrong. This wasn't a result of her being too busy and doing too many things. She needed answers.

After years of living in the unknown, she found herself back at the doctor's office, one doctor after another, desperate now to find the answers that were not given to her before. Lots of tests and blood work followed. Slivers of hope coupled with frustration were felt when the first two tests came back negative—relief to not have those diseases, but what did she have? When the third test came back positive, everything changed. Life stopped and stood still for what seemed like forever.

"Lori, you have lupus. I am so sorry."

What? How could this be her story? How could this be possible? She was only 24 years old, a young bride, and a new mom. This was supposed to be the prime of her life. Her best years were supposed to be ahead for her, but now what? Fear crippled her heart like the pain had crippled her hands. Tears ran down her face. "God, please change this. Make this go away. Don't let this be true. Don't let this be my story."

For all she knew, she had just received a death sentence without a date. Sadness and fear were her new companions. Her body was failing her, and she didn't know why. She knew little about this disease and its ramifications. Receiving the news at work, she went straight to her friend who worked in the pharmacy, hopeful that she might be able to shed some light on her diagnosis. "It can't possibly be that. Don't worry, Lori." A bit of hope re-entered her heart. Maybe it wasn't true. Maybe this wouldn't be her story after all.

Despite the wishful thinking of others and her hopes that this was just all a bad dream, her diagnosis of lupus was confirmed. Refusing to spend the rest of her life in fear of the unknown, she started to research the disease. Her research was coupled with more doctors' appointments. The more she learned about lupus, the more dread and hope filled her heart. She fell on the mild end of the spectrum, and she also learned that it's not a disease that necessarily gets progressively worse. Good news, right? Well, that knowledge came with some other information. While the doctors had found it in her early on and her case was considered "mild," there remained much unknown.

In many ways, lupus remains a mystery in modern medicine. It's a disease that behaves differently in each of its hosts, and it's hard to judge what it will do next. It jumps around the body, attacking different parts at different times without warning or remorse. This unknown is what awaited her.

Her new normal became a daily regimen of medications and lots of doctors' appointments and more tests, and with this new normal came its own side effects, some irreversible. She started to feel better fairly quickly with the new medications, but she was given no certainty that these painful flare ups wouldn't come back. And they did come back. Were the medications even working? Was it worth the risk of all of the potential side effects that could be had from taking the medications if she couldn't even be certain that they were helping?

Each time her lupus would rear its ugly head affecting a different part of her body, no answers could ever seem to be found on how to cure the symptoms or take away the pain. Frustration filled her thoughts. Feelings of hopelessness and weariness filled her heart. How was she going to live this way for the rest of her life? How could she face each day with such pain and discomfort?

Somehow, hope remained in the midst of the fear and the loss of dreams. A hope that was deeply rooted in the fabric of her being began to strengthen and grow in the face of adversity. She had faith in a God who was not moved by this terrible disease. She had faith in a God who was bigger than lupus could ever be. She had faith in a God who is Healer. She had faith in a God who may choose not to heal her, but she knew that even if He didn't, He would still be good and that He would use this for good. Her hope began to embrace what she had been entrusted with.

The cycles of her lupus have never been easy, and it has remained a hard fought battle to possess and maintain the hope she still clings to. Breathing issues, digestive issues, more excruciating pain followed, and the cycle kept going. Life seemed to be spinning out of control, and with the spinning, there were more and more doctors, more unanswered questions, more and more unknown. Tests and tests and more tests. Lots of fear. "It's just your lupus," they would say.

Even so, somehow, someway, she would always go back to these words of faith: "God is in control, and there's a reason why these things are happening." She describes it all like a big puzzle. "Everything that happens in this life is a small puzzle piece in a huge puzzle. We try to figure it out, but we can't see the whole puzzle. God sees the whole puzzle, and He knows where each piece is supposed to go."

Her battle for hope in the hopelessness of her illness was up and down. She would stand firm and remain in places of faith, trusting God in the unknown, but then she'd receive another blow to her health. She grew so weary of doctors, tests, spending so much money, and never getting any answers. So, she just stopped. The endless tests and examinations were proving to be fruitless, only causing her more stress and frustration with the lack of answers that they would bring. So, she stopped. She stopped exhausting herself with countless doctors and medications.

The lupus hasn't gone away. At times, it feels as if it's gotten worse, and at other times, there seems to be some relief. That is the nature of the disease. Rheumatoid arthritis has now been added to the list of her ailments, and the pain of arthritis has spread throughout her whole body. Pain is a part of her days. Exhaustion remains her foe. Surprise flare ups come and go.

Still, she has not lost hope, because her hope is in the Lord. Does she hope for healing and believe for it to come? You bet she does. Does she know beyond a shadow of a doubt that God is able to restore her body to perfect health and wholeness? Absolutely. She has not lost hope in God's ability, and she never will. He has been too faithful thus far for her to walk away now. She has done everything that she can to find healing for herself, but she knows that her healing ultimately rests in the hands of Jesus. Whether it is realized on this side of heaven or the other, her hope embraces the journey God has her on today.

She's gone through many disheartening moments throughout this process. She has days when she is an emotional wreck—days when she has no idea how she's going to make it through—but then she comes back to hope. "God can do this. God can heal me. God's going to do this." She doesn't know when. She doesn't know how, but she believes and has so much hope in the face of a seemingly hopeless situation. The holistic program she has been on is coming to an end, and she's not where she had hoped to be. Even so, she's already looking forward to the next thing, the next potential road to her healing, and she is going to do everything she can to find it and to trust God to do the miraculous.

The last nine plus years of her life have been marked by lupus, and the past three years have been marked by constant pain. The good days are sprinkled in between lots of bad days. It's been so painful and so hard, and there isn't an end in sight.

But God.

Her hope embraces who He is in the midst of what her body has become. She doesn't live 100% of the time in a place of hope, but she always finds herself returning there. It's been too hard for too long for her to not know that God is going to do something great through this. She hopes for healing, but she also knows that physical healing may not be the answer. What she is confident of is this: God uses everything that happens for our good and for His glory. Her biggest hope, even beyond hope for healing, is that God would use her story of pain. She can't even imagine the greatness that God has in store— that all of her pain and suffering would be worth it for the amazing puzzle that He is putting together and each piece of her story and pain is a part of the greater picture He is creating. She knows that God is good and faithful in all that He does, so her hope embraces her story. Her hope embraces her God. Through it all, God will be seen. Through it all, God will be glorified. Through it all, God will be known.

CHAPTER 5

HOPE IGNITES

I WAS GIVEN the privilege this past year to sit in a room of nearly 1000 women who do what I do. It was an invitation I could not refuse, and it was an opportunity for me unlike any other. This room was filled with leaders in ministry who spend their days, and more importantly, their lives, building the Kingdom of God here on this earth. Through writing, speaking, and worship leading, these female leaders are changing the course of Kingdom history one faithful and obedient step at a time, and I was beyond blessed to sit among them.

The less than 24 hours we were given to spend together has proven to be such a valuable investment in my life, and the fruit that was produced within me from our time together is simply immeasurable. I was encouraged. I was equipped. I was empowered. I was inspired. There is something so incredibly life giving about being in the presence of those who carry hope. It had this effect to breed hope in me.

Hope has this insane ability to produce hope in others. Hope begets hope. Hope cannot help but to foster hope in the hearts of others because hope ignites more hope. It's in the very nature of hope to do so. Hope was never meant to be contained, but like a wildfire out of control, it was intended to spread. To know hope is to inevitably breed hope in others.

It falls in step with the love of Christ. God's love is far too high and deep and long and wide to be contained by only a few. It was never intended to be hoarded or reserved like food in a famine. The reaches of God's love have always been intended to know no bounds. There is no end or limit to the love of God, and the same can be said of hope. Because hope cannot be disconnected from the person and work of Jesus Christ, when it is had and known, it spreads. The hope-filled person can do nothing but spread the hope which they have received in Christ because true hope will always flow from every aspect of who they are.

We work hard to compartmentalize our lives, believing that there is much benefit from doing so. However, the result of such living produces little more than a divided heart, and we find ourselves desperate for hope when, in fact, it has always been ours for the taking. We section off our lives, only allowing God into certain parts while keeping Him from entering into other parts. One who knows hope also knows that every part of life is to be brought before the Lord in surrender—every single part. Nothing is to be withheld. It is that act of complete and full surrender that invites hope to readily flow, and when hope flows so freely, the overflow pours out onto everyone with whom we come into contact. It can't be stopped. It can't be contained.

> *May the God of hope fill you with all joy and peace as you trust in Him, so that you may overflow with hope by the power of the Holy Spirit.*
>
> Romans 15:13

I love the words of this prayer. The apostle Paul penned them thousands of years ago, but the inspiration of the Holy Spirit that backs them allows these same words to ring just as powerfully and just as true today. As he begins to wrap up his letter to the Romans, Paul sprinkles powerful prayers like this one throughout his writing. He writes words of instruction and conviction, and then, just like a loving pastor would do for his flock, he encourages them with words of hope and truth.

Can you see how our definition of hope is woven throughout the words of this short prayer? **Hope is a strong and confident expectation, an unwavering trust in the unchanging character of God.** As we trust in God, He deposits His hope into our hearts. Hope is intrinsically linked to trust. We know this. We know this. We see it throughout Scripture. That very hope that He gives us has the effect of igniting hope in others. If we have His hope within us, it will overflow from us.

Just sit in this space for a bit longer and reflect on hope with me. When is the last time you sat in the presence of a hope-filled person? What effect did their hope have on you? As you watched them respond to their own circumstances, whether good or bad circumstances, what about their response impacted you the most? Was it their ability to have hope in the face of daunting trials and hardship that moved you toward hope yourself? Was it their steadiness and stability that blew you away?

As I sat in that room, surrounded by other women in ministry, hope flooded my heart. I had been in a long season of difficulty, and to be honest, I find that I am still in it. However, I sat and listened to women of faith who have been leading in ministry for longer than I have been alive. As they humbly and authentically shared with us about many of the trials they had been through, hope sparked a flame within my soul once again. These women who have spiritually led me from a distance for years breathed life into our bones that day as they openly shared both their victories and defeats. They told us of their own experiences of despair and heartache in ministry, a world which we so often falsely believe is immune to those pains. They didn't end the story there, though. They pushed past the hurt, with us as their captivated audience, to share with us the unshakeable hope they have in our Savior.

People will fail us. We know this. People will betray us and even seek to destroy our name. We have, unfortunately, experienced this. But our God will not fail us. Our God will never betray us. We can be confident of this. These pillars of faith, these women whom I have revered for years, became incredibly human to me that day as I sat among my peers. They hurt, just as I do. When you cut them, they bleed red, just like I do. Words wound them, just as they wound me. They are required to put their hope in the Lord and not in man, just as I am. When hope is rightly placed in the Lord, it ignites hope in others. It ignited hope in me that day.

Hope anchors us. Paul, despite the persecution he endured for the name of Jesus, had an unshakable hope that carried him all the way through to his own martyr's death. Nothing, not even the threat of death itself, could steal the hope upon which Paul had built his life. Refusing to cower in fear, Paul chose hope, which ignited strength and courage within him to rise to every occasion and opportunity to breed hope in others. He knew that hope was found alone in the name of Jesus, so he spread the hope he had found in that name. He knew no better way to live than to live hope filled.

Can you and I say the same? Can we, with just as much conviction, declare that there is no better way to live than to live in Christ? Do our lives proclaim that truth, or do they refute it? Are our attempts at achieving happiness actually robbing us of true joy, peace, and hope? We keep climbing all of these ladders that promise fulfillment once we reach the top of them, but what we keep realizing at each summit is nothing more than the fact that these ladders are leaning against the wrong wall. We keep staking our lives on value systems that don't line up with the Word of God, and we then wonder why hope seems to escape us. If we're after hope, then we need to go to the source. "The God of hope" that Romans 15:13 speaks of is where hope will be found. When we lean our ladders against that wall, we will not be disappointed in the climb. Every step we take on that journey will prove to deposit more hope into our souls. The more hope we receive, the more hope others around us will experience, because hope ignites hope.

Let's take one more look at Romans 15:13. This verse closes with a phrase that I do not want any of us to miss: ***"by the power of the Holy Spirit."*** Lest we think for even a moment that any of this hope talk is possible on our own, let's be reassured that this hope is had, known, and ignited in others by the power of the Holy Spirit. This is not our doing. This is a supernatural work done with supernatural power. We aren't the ones to receive the glory for the work, because we aren't the ones doing the work. Likewise, we need not grow weary in the process, because it's not a process which we are responsible for initiating or completing. "The God of hope" begins the work within us, and the work is completed in us and poured out into others "by the power of the Holy Spirit."

There is much freedom to be realized in this truth. All we have to do is live in the hope which we have been given. That's it. Live in hope. Our hope is in Jesus Christ. He is the founder of our hope. He is the initiator of our hope. He is the sustainer of our hope. He is the ignitor of our hope, and praise be to God, He will one day complete our hope in Him. As followers of Jesus Christ, we have much to anticipate, much to look forward to. The road to our eternal destination will be long, and it will prove to be difficult, but the end of our story is victorious.

So, we fix our eyes on Jesus, the author and perfecter of our faith. We keep walking forward with hope intact. We continue to move in the rhythms of God's grace. Hope anchors our soul. Hope tethers us to a God who does not waiver. Eternity is written on our hearts. Heaven is our home. He will complete the work He began in us, and it will be to the praise and glory of His name.

I have not always been found in places of hope, but I am learning to be. The temptation to despair in the face of trial remains present and strong, but as I position myself more and more at the feet of Jesus, I am finding a community of hope there. Among this community of hope, I have found freedom. I watch as others are being pulled further and further from places of despair and hopeless living, and it is breeding hope in me. Hope is being found, and hope is igniting more hope within my soul.

We were made for so much more than hopeless living. Jesus didn't bear that brutal cross so that you and I would carry on in defeat. He did not conquer sin and the grave so that we would live in despair. He is our victorious King so that we, too, can live in victory. So, are we choosing to live in victory?

Lean into the truth today that hope is yours for the taking. Choose to look past the brokenness of your own story to see the hope that awaits you—the hope of Jesus Christ. Hope is for you, hope is with you, and hope ignites hope. Allow the Word of God and the word of Bristi's testimony to spark hope within you. Hope has been worth every step of the journey.

This is her hope story.

Bristi was 25 when she first met him. Although she had been raised in a Christian home, had known about who God was, and had spent much time in the church world, she had long since departed walking the walk of faith. It had never really set in. She was finding much more pleasure in living life for herself. Boundaries and restrictions were a thing of her past. Her present was all about fun. Bars, drinking, living the nightlife. That was her life.

So, when she first met him, her filters were not really in place. At first glance, he seemed like everything she had ever wanted and more. Attractive. Fun. Liked to have a good time. What more could she want in this season of her life?

Abuse comes in all forms, though, and it can often begin very subtly. At first, it started with comments about her appearance. "If you were thinner, if you were taller, then I could really see us together." His words were like a dagger in her heart. The constant negative feedback about her looks, weight, and appearance cut deeper than she could have even imagined. What began as a slow unraveling would take years to mend.

But she cared for him, and he said he cared for her, or at least he could care for her if certain things about her changed. So, she purged what she ate, became obsessed with her figure, and wore high heels wherever they went. She was desperately trying to fit the mold he had demanded for her to fit into, but it wore on her. The lies he was feeding her about herself were becoming her new truth. Maybe she wasn't good enough. Maybe she didn't deserve him. Maybe, maybe, maybe.

So is the nature of abuse. It starts with the heart and

emotions. Once that part is under control, the abuser can take it to a whole new level. That is exactly what he did. The first year of their dating relationship, they lived several hours from each other, but would travel to see each other often. It was on one of those fateful trips that she caught him cheating on her. If only it had been one time. But it wasn't.

Some might think that this would have been the perfect time for her to get out, but he already had her in his grip. "No one else will ever love you. You don't even deserve me." So she stayed, believing the lies, succumbing to more and more abuse.

Drinking, cheating, verbal and physical abuse, threats, and more had become the cycle of their relationship, but what could she do now? Despite every red flag, when he proposed, she said "yes" in hopes that perhaps this would change him, but marriage quickly proved to be worse than what she had experienced with him before.

The ongoing abuse in their marriage, coupled with repeated counts of unfaithfulness on his part, landed them in counseling, something she desperately wanted to work for their marriage, but something in which he was not at all interested. In fact, the accountability of a counselor did not even cause the verbal abuse to stop. "If she were thinner, then I would give her the love that she wants." Despite the downward spiral, marriage brought them a baby boy—the one ray of hope, the tangible expression of God's grace to her in the darkest time of her life.

Pregnancy can have a way of changing a woman, and forcing her to come to grip with her priorities. She knew she didn't want her son to live life apart from God like she had for so many years. The pull back to God almost felt like a gravitational force, and she found herself back in church again, learning, growing, and eventually serving. All the while, life at home hadn't changed. If nothing else, it had only grown worse. When the next affair became public, she was removed from her leadership position at church. The shame of his sin seemed to now be placed on her shoulders. What could she do?

Brokenness has a way of forcing us to look up. When we truly hit rock bottom, there is no where else to look but up. So, she did. In the wake of further emotional devastation in her marriage, and hurt from the church where she had begun to grow in her walk with the Lord, she found a small group of women who wanted to go through a Bible study on the book of Ephesians. She joined. As she immersed herself in the Word of God, she began to find the hope and healing that had been absent from her life for so long. God's Word was a salve to her wounds.

God's faithfulness began to illuminate itself throughout her life, even in the midst of the fiercest storm. She found a new church home, continued to study Ephesians with these women, and regularly met with her counselor. These three key ingredients would prove to be the recipe for freedom in her life.

As her faith in Christ grew, so did her resolve. She had decided she was going to leave him, but it needed to be done very carefully. He had already made it very clear to her what the consequences would be if she ever tried to leave him, and those consequences were very permanent. "If you ever leave me, I will bury you in a field, and no one will ever find you."

Even in this darkness, God had brought into her life an amazing amount of faith-filled people who were ready to support her in this exodus. They helped her plan. They helped her pack. Over the course of a few months, they would slowly move her things out while he was away at work. His constant state of drunkenness never afforded him the ability to even notice. Then the day finally came, one Sunday after Christmas. She left him a letter, packed the rest of her things, and drove the six hours home with a dear and trusted friend. She was finally free of him. She and her son were gone.

Of course, this wasn't the end of the story. The threats continued, which were almost always immediately followed by promises. "If you don't come back to me, I will find you." "Bristi, I love you. I promise to change. I will give you the world and more. Just come home." She was wiser now, though. She could see straight through it, and she wasn't about to return to that old life. God had begun to pave a new, beautiful road for her, one which she couldn't even fully see yet.

Now, a single mom who for the past several years had not worked outside of the home, Bristi found herself without any other option but to trust that God would provide for her needs. It's amazing how our trust in God so often seems to ignite His provision in our lives. She had taken a giant leap of faith in leaving her husband, trusting that this was what she was supposed to do, and now she was desperate for God to show up and prove His faithfulness in her life. And that is exactly what He did, again and again and again.

Every financial need, down to the dollar, was covered month after month. Bills were paid. Food was on the table. She was amazed at how detailed God was in His provision toward her, down to the extra $15 a month she had to spare. God even provided a way for her to work from home, running her own makeup business so that she could be home with her young son. As she continued to walk in faithfulness, God kept showing up and blessing her immeasurably more than she could even think to ask for or imagine.

The study of Ephesians had truly changed her life. God had opened her eyes to so much truth in this one Bible study that she kept going through it again. The more she learned about who God says He is and who God said she was in His Word, the more hope and faith spilled out of her onto the others around her. Her business was really taking off, and she was building a team of women and supporting them in their own businesses. They became the recipients of her newfound hope and faith. The hope in her was like a magnet, attracting anyone within a five-foot radius to her. They wanted what she had. When she shared about the hope she had found in Jesus, they wanted to know how she had found it.

A Bible study on the book of Ephesians that began with just four women meeting in a living room turned into almost 2000 women spanning across the United States and in three different countries around the world studying the book of Ephesians with her because of her faithfulness, courage, and refusal to hold back the hope that had been deposited into her heart.

Bristi is a world changer. In the middle of what she would describe as the hardest, darkest season of her life, God was drawing her back to Him. With certainty and full conviction, she would tell you today that she would go through it all again because that broken road led her straight to the arms of her Savior. The journey was hard and incredibly painful. There was much loss along the way, and there is still a daily fight that remains to put on the mind of Christ and to think His thoughts about herself instead of the lies, but now she is full of hope. Her hope abounds. Her new reality is a strong and confident expectation, an unwavering trust in the unchanging character of God. This hope is now hers, and she cannot help herself from sharing it with anyone who will get close enough to listen.

Hope ignites. Hope begets hope. Hope calls out hope in others. This is her hope story.

Tethered to an Unwavering God in the Depths

CHAPTER 6
HOPELESS

CALLING ALL THE hopeless, the downcast, the despondent, the weary, those who carry heavy burdens, those with weak and feeble knees. Will you lend me your ear for these next few pages? Will you lean into the pain with me and these words long enough to gain an understanding of its purpose in your life? Will you get into the trenches of despair with me? Will you learn alongside me?

By definition, hopeless means "to be without hope, having no hope, despairing, desperate." Just reading those words as I type them conjures up within me a distinct remembrance of what it felt like to be in those places of hopelessness. To be hopeless is one of the least desirable places I can imagine. I've been there, and I never want to return.

If we adhere to our biblical definition of hope, understanding that hope is entirely connected to Jesus Christ because He is our hope, then we can conclude that to be truly hopeless is to be without God, and to be without the life that Jesus Christ provides. Have you ever been there—without God and therefore, without hope in this world?

We all should be able to answer "yes" to that question, because not a single one of us was born a Christ follower. We were not born Christian. We may have been given the gift of being born into a God-loving, Christian home, but our inherited DNA from our parents did not include our salvation. That was a decision we made on our own to accept the free gift of the grace of God. There was a moment in time, a choice made, a surrender that took place when we finally said "yes" to Jesus' call.

When was this moment for you? Have you had this moment yet? I ask because hope hinges on your response.

The book of Ephesians has always been a part of Scripture that draws me in repeatedly. I love the message of this book. I love the call to "Awake, O Sleeper" and to start living like a Christian if you say you are one. I love the honesty and truth. I love the prayers recorded within from the Apostle Paul. I love the promises given. I love how much of our identity can be found and learned within its few short pages. Still, there is another part I love within the book of Ephesians. It's a part that might surprise you. It's the hard and honest truth. This type of truth can be difficult for us to swallow. These are the portions of Scripture we might just prefer to leave right there on the page instead of allowing them to penetrate our hearts.

But God's Word is not a buffet.

Did you know that? While we often approach it as such, taking extra portions of the parts that make us feel good while leaving the rest behind for someone else, it is not a buffet. We don't get to pick and choose which parts of God's Word are true. It is entirely true, completely inspired, wholly inerrant, and the very breath and words of God on the pages. That makes every word good, whether we like them or not.

On that note, let's take a look at one such passage in the book of Ephesians, a particular section of Scripture that I read through and passed by for years—until God arrested me with the powerful truth found within these verses. Ephesians chapter two might appear to be a joy zapper for some who approach God's Word only looking for a pat on the back, a "Good job! Keep up the good work," or the warm fuzzy feelings that the "good parts" often provide. What I have found, though, is that joy can be found, kept, and known in all parts of Scripture, even the more difficult sections to digest.

Why is Ephesians 2 so hard to swallow? It tells us in great detail the honest truth about you and about me before we were "in Christ." That two word phrase "in

Christ" is found numerous times throughout Ephesians. It is referring to our spiritual identity, our new heritage, the status of our relationship with God. To be "in Christ" is to be all that God says you are. To be "in Christ" is to be made new and covered in God's grace. To be "in Christ" is to be the new creation that is no longer marked by the foolish ways of this world. That is what it means to be in Christ.

Ephesians 2 tells us all about what our lives looked like and how much we lacked before we were in Christ. It paints an incredibly true but uncomfortable picture of our spiritual condition, and what is interesting to me is that it has everything to do with hope.

> *And you were dead in the trespasses and sins in which you once walked, following the course of this world, following the prince of the power of the air, the spirit that is now at work in the sons of disobedience—among whom we all once lived in the passions of our flesh, carrying out the desires of the body and the mind, and were by nature children of wrath, like the rest of mankind.*
>
> Ephesians 2:1-3

Talk about a hopeless state. In case you missed it, the descriptions given of us before we were in Christ are as follows: dead in sin, followers of the world, disobedient, living for our own passions and desires, and children of wrath.

That is heavy. In short, there was no good to be found in us apart from Christ. Nothing. That is hopelessness. Think back to your own days before you gave your life to Jesus. Maybe you don't have to think back very far. Maybe those days are your current days. The first step toward hope-filled living is to start seeing things through God's eyes. When we can begin to connect our hopelessness to Scripture and what it has to say about our spiritual condition, we begin to move ourselves in the right direction. It doesn't end in verse three, though.

I'm going to jump ahead in chapter two to complete this thought we began about hopelessness. Hopeless living is meant for life outside of Christ, not for life in Christ. Paul goes on to explain in even further detail and description what our lives looked like before we were rescued by God's grace.

> *... remember that you were at that time separated from Christ, alienated from the commonwealth of Israel and strangers to the covenants of promise, having no hope and without God in the*

world.

Ephesians 2:12

Notice how the phrase "having no hope" is immediately followed by "and without God in the world." Do you want to know why? They are intricately linked. You cannot separate the two. If we hold to our biblical definition of hope, then to be without hope means to be without God in this world, to be separated from Him, alienated from His blessings, strangers to His promises, and having no hope. It is a condition with which you and I were once familiar. The sinful nature we were born into resists God. In our resistance of God, we forfeited our hope. Every time we choose to elevate the things of this world over the things of our God, our hope becomes misplaced. Misplaced hope eventually becomes hopelessness. Oh, but friends, this is not where the story ends. Let's look back on some of those verses we skipped.

> *But God, being rich in mercy, because of the great love with which he loved us, even when we were dead in our trespasses, made us alive together with Christ—by grace you have been saved— and raised us up with him and seated us with him in the heavenly places in Christ Jesus, so that in the coming ages he might show the immeasurable riches of*

*his grace in kindness toward us in Christ
Jesus. For by grace you have been saved
through faith. And this is not your own
doing; it is the gift of God, not a result
of works, so that no one may boast.
For we are his workmanship, created in
Christ Jesus for good works, which God
prepared beforehand, that we should
walk in them.*

Ephesians 2:4-10

There are some glorious interjections in Scripture,
some very beautiful "buts." We have one right here in
Ephesians 2:4 when it says, "But God …" After all of
the hard and honest truth of the first three verses—the
hopeless condition of our souls apart from Christ—we
are given some rich hope in verse four. It is because of
God's mercy and grace alone that we can transfer from
the valleys of hopelessness to the pastures of hope that
He has for us. It was His great mercy and sovereign
grace that rescued us from the pits of hopeless living.
Hopelessness is connected to our lives apart from
Jesus. Once we are in Christ, this is what becomes our
reality according to Ephesians 2:4-10: We are made alive,
we are saved, we are raised, we are seated with Him, we
are the recipients of His kindness, we don't have to earn
it or sustain it because it's free, we are His workmanship,
and good works await us in Him.

That's a mouthful of blessing. That is ample reason for hope. That is an enormous amount of promise, and it is all ours in Christ. Hope can be had for you, and hope can be had for me. This promise of hope fulfilled is found in Christ alone. Hopeless living is not for the children of God. Difficult times, hardships, and trials of many kinds? Yes, those are to be expected for us as God's children, but hopelessness need not accompany them. The deepest depths of hopeless living can be tasted outside of the saving relationship with Jesus Christ, but friends, it should not be known within it. Hope is our inheritance in Christ. Hope is our song. Hope is our assurance.

Hope is a person, and His name is Jesus.

To the hopeless, downcast, despondent, weary, burdened, and weak sojourner: Do you know the grace of Jesus Christ? Have you received it for yourself? This one free gift of mercy and grace will rewrite your story. It will turn your sorrow into dancing. It will make beauty from your ashes. It will take your hopelessness and in exchange, give you lasting hope. His Word is true. His promise is true. This is my testimony. I am living proof, and so is Lindsay.

This is her hope story.

Lindsay was the perfect candidate, as some might say. She was raised in a Christian home, went to church several times a week, loved Jesus, and surrounded herself with Christian friends. Who wouldn't have thought that this girl was on the path of hope-filled living? Her love for God kept compelling her toward wanting more and more of Him. Church involvement didn't seem to be enough for her. She wanted to be immersed in a Christian environment every day of the week. Christian school felt like the obvious choice, but she quickly came to find out that it was simply not an option for her family. So, they pursued what seemed to be the second best option: a charter school that had come highly recommended by some close, Christian friends. While not a faith-based school, Lindsay walked into it with high hopes of finding more of Jesus there than she had at her previous school.

Her high hopes were quickly brought low when she realized that she was not in the environment that she had hoped for. Why had their friends recommended this school? The influences here seemed worse than at her previous school. How was this place going to propel her forward in her faith?

Determined to make a difference, she prioritized her faith in this new world which only seemed to mock it. She even joined a student ministry, but it didn't take long before she began to grow tired of standing alone in her faith. Swimming upstream was proving to be far more difficult than just going with the flow.

It started slowly at first. One compromise here, another compromise there. But this slow fade led to a downward spiral from which she could not find an easy way out. Drinking and drugs became the new normal for her on the weekends, and what started as something that was infrequent became more and more frequent, until she could no longer separate these behaviors from who she was becoming. Church attendance for her and her family was now a thing of the past, and the light of hope she had once carried seemed to be only a distant memory.

Life continued this way for some time, but Lindsay never for one minute believed that any of this had gotten out of control. She still believed in God. She would have told you that she still loved God, but she wasn't living for God. While she slowly chipped away at who she was, a new numbing began to take up residence in her heart, causing her to believe far less of herself than who she was created to be.

As she entered college, she met and quickly fell for her first love. With most of her other convictions now long gone, she gave her whole self to this boy. Tainted. No longer pure. At least, that's how she saw herself. Since she had given herself to this guy, she felt that she had to stay with him, despite all the warning signs.

A recovering heroine addict.
An abusive man.

Addicted to prescription pills.
Just to name a few.

But then, there was his good side. He wanted to go to church with her. When her grandpa died, he wanted to help console her. So, he brought her his own coping mechanism. Pills. Her first high. After that, more and more pills. It's interesting the nature of sin. It over-promises, but it under-delivers, every time. Pills promised a temporary high that would allow her to escape the pain of loss that she didn't know how to deal with, but once that high was gone, she needed more. When pills were no longer enough, she then turned to heroine. Hooked. Addicted.

Addiction had taken over. She had allowed this darkness into her life, and she was beginning to see how it was making her a different person. The downward spiral continued.

When this abusive, toxic relationship ended, she was left alone with a terrible addiction, one she couldn't seem to overcome. Her craving for another high kept leading her to people and places that only perpetuated the darkness inside of her. It was only a matter of time before she had lost everything. Homeless. Jobless. Hungry. Addicted. It was four years of this struggle, this total addiction, this hitting rock bottom again and again before she woke up to the reality that if she didn't get help, she was going to die.

Her first three months in the recovery program with the Salvation Army seemed like it was going to be her road back home. She was detoxing, and finally getting back on her feet. Until she slipped. What had started as a determination and commitment to get off drugs and off the streets turned into a night of absolute terror for her that she'll never forget. One bad decision coupled with one bad acquaintance whom she had met in the program, and she found herself leaving the program for a night of fun. Drugs, overdoses, CPR, near death.

"Lindsay, what are you doing? You were clean, and now this?" Her thoughts raced inside her mind, and she knew that if she didn't get serious about her recovery, she was never going to recover. She needed a new environment, different people, a new commitment.

The Salvation Army program in Colorado seemed very promising to her. It was a much longer program, but this time, she was absolutely determined to defeat this darkness that had stolen so much of her life. While her friends were off graduating from college, she was graduating from a drug rehab program. Still, she was proud of herself. She had put in six months of faith-based learning, detoxing, and ultimately life change in this program, and she decided to stay on for another three months, because she loved it so much there. She had not only grown out of the addiction, but she had grown into a genuine, saving relationship with Jesus.

True hope finally began to flood her heart and mind as she pictured her future free of addiction.

When she first met Zach, she was leery about being in a relationship so soon into her recovery, but they quickly became inseparable and each other's new addictions. Plus, dating in the program was not encouraged. It's just too easy for the recovering addict to quickly become addicted to something or someone else. Still, she couldn't help but follow her heart, and what felt like a promising relationship between two recovering heroine addicts slowly began to take a turn for the worse. Church and program attendance went out the window. With those pieces of accountability gone, they found themselves vulnerable to their own weaknesses. Alcohol was reintroduced into their lives, but they justified it because, "It wasn't heroine." Old friends from his days before recovery were also reintroduced, and the warning signs continued to light up in Lindsay's heart.

With the re-entry of old habits and old friends, addiction lurked around the corner. While Lindsay's guard was high, Zach's was not. Within a few weeks of losing two close friends to drug overdose, Lindsay found out that she was pregnant. And life just stopped. As she looked back on the past year of her life, she longed for the freedom she and Zach once knew, but as she stared at the present, she couldn't help but see disaster in their future if they didn't change. If he didn't change.

A few months pregnant and a few ultimatums later, Lindsay packed her bags to return to Arizona, leaving Zach in Colorado to think about his current state of affairs. It was the hardest decision she ever made, but she knew she had to do it. She could stay with him, knowing how that road back to addiction would look, knowing that their own child would be taken from their arms if they kept going down that road together, or she could leave and hope that her exodus would be the final straw that would turn Zach around in the right direction.

Months of fighting over the phone and long hard conversations followed. Could she still hold onto hope? But then, against all hope, Zach came for the birth of their daughter, Zaylyn, and things started to look a bit more promising than she had thought. Could they really be a family again? Could they stay the course this time?

She certainly thought so. Her hope brought her back to Colorado for a season of trying to reestablish what had been broken. Until his addiction reared its ugly head one final time. She knew she couldn't live like this anymore. She knew she couldn't raise her daughter like this. She knew she wanted the life of freedom in Christ more than she wanted this. So, she left one last time. And he didn't follow her.

Months went by, and their daughter had almost reached her first birthday when she received the fateful call.

Zach had overdosed on heroine. Any dreams of hope she had once clung to came crashing down around her. Days turned into endless nights for her. Joy, even in her daughter, turned to depression. She slept her days away. Hopelessness was her only companion. Despair. Darkness. No hope.

Hospitalization. Medication after medication. Nothing was working. She felt so defeated, so hopeless. One night, she picked up the phone and called the suicide hotline. Her last resort. Somehow, she was disconnected. What? Of all times for her phone to not work, this was the worst time. In the stillness of that dark moment, she heard God's voice calling out to her.

"Call me."

Sobbing and crying out to the God of her youth on her hands and knees on the living room floor, she invited God back into her story. Words simply cannot capture what occurred next. While weeping and sorrow may last for the night, joy comes in the morning. (Psalm 30:5) She woke the next day with hope in her heart, a hope she had never felt or known in her life before that day. While it wasn't an overnight, 100% turnaround, God had recaptured her heart that night, and she began walking down new paths that He was setting out before her.

God helped her find the perfect counselor who helped

walk her through complete healing and freedom from her painful, broken, and addicted past. A Bible-believing, Christian church helped her connect with godly community, something she hadn't experienced in so long. Hopelessness was her past. Hope became her story.

God kept putting it on her heart that she needed to share her story. So, she took some frightened but faith-filled steps forward in doing just that: sharing her story. She was finding hope, peace, and purpose in Christ. As she was learning to grow in Christ, trust and surrender followed.

It's been two years of walking with Jesus, trusting Him on the journey of learning to let go, and the beauty in surrender. She has such faith and hope in the God who saved her life and rescued her soul. She is free. Hope is her new story. She tried for so long to fill this God-sized hole with everything but God. Now that she's filling it with Him, she can't get enough of Him. To be in her presence is truly refreshing and deposits hope into my own heart. She has been purified, made new. She is so grateful.

From the depths of despair to the heights of hope, this is Lindsay's hope story.

CHAPTER 7

HOPE ILLUMINATES

THERE IS SOMETHING about a candle glowing in a dark room that just captivates me. I've always been mesmerized by fire. There is a fierceness to it and a power that it holds that is almost enchanting. Its warmth is inviting. Its glow secures my gaze. I could stare at a flame for hours on end, never shifting my eyes from the blaze.

I love a room that is illuminated by only candlelight. Every other light in the house could be turned off, but that one candle's burning flame has the ability to bring light into the darkness. Its ability to illuminate what you otherwise wouldn't be able to see so intrigues me. A small flame can shed light on an enormous space, bringing clarity of vision with it.

It's not surprising to me that Jesus described Himself as a light. His light was the light of truth—a light that opened spiritually blind eyes to see. Wherever Jesus went, He brought the light of truth with Him. Whenever He opened His mouth, truth flowed from His lips, illuminating the spiritual darkness around Him. A light illuminates the darkness, and it has the ability to expose what lingers in the darkness. Whatever is in the dark cannot escape the light. It's impossible. Light illuminates.

> *Again Jesus spoke to them, saying, "I am the light of the world. Whoever follows me will not walk in darkness, but will have the light of life.*
>
> John 8:12

It's amazing, isn't it? To follow Jesus, to pursue His truth, and to be found in relationship with Him is to walk in the light. To walk in the light is to effectively expel the darkness. The light of Christ expels the darkness within you, and it also expels the darkness around you. Our biblical understanding of hope has the same effect. Hope, a strong and confident expectation, an unwavering trust in the unchanging character of God, illuminates the darkness that so often seeks to envelope and engulf us, the darkness that blinds us.

I don't know what you believe to be true about God. I'm not sure how the events and details of your story have shaped your understanding of Scripture. I have no idea what kind of darkness you are experiencing in your own life right now, but may I present you with an invitation, today? Could I invite you to the light, the flame of truth, that will illuminate all darkness?

Our journey today will be one of pursuing truth in order to expel the darkness. We will sit with the pages of Scripture and allow God's Word to reshape our thinking and our belief systems. As we expose ourselves to the light of His truth, may whatever darkness that resides in or around us be sent to flight. I am after some hope for us today because hope illuminates.

> *Where can I go from your Spirit? Where can I flee from your presence?*
>
> Psalm 139:7

I find our inability to escape the ever watchful eye of the Lord quite comforting. Does it also bring a sense of holy fear, reverence, and awe? Sure, it does, but there is hope to be found in a God who is never absent, even when I have tried to run from Him. At one point or another, we all have tried to hide from His all-seeing eyes. It started in the Garden of Eden and it, unfortunately, continues today. In our pursuit of temporal things, we so easily forget His eternal nature—that He is omniscient and omnipresent. Run as we may, we could never outrun the Lord. His love will always run faster than our sin ever could.

The psalmist captures so eloquently here what many of us struggle to put into words. For those of us who have spent any amount of time wandering from the Lord, we know these words of Psalm 139 to be true. Jesus finds the one lost sheep every time. He pursues after the wanderer. He's so good at it. There isn't a place in this vast universe where we could go that would escape His presence. He's already there.

> *If I go up to the heavens, you are there; if I make my bed in the depths, you are there. If I rise on the wings of the dawn, if I settle on the far side of the sea, even there your hand will guide me, your right hand will hold me fast.*

Psalm 139:8-10

Just in case we managed to miss the point in verse 7, the same truth is reiterated here again for us to read. Not only will His presence be in each of these places, but we will be met with His guidance there, as well. When we run from Him, He'll beat us to our destination, welcome us when we finally arrive, and He'll hold us in the palm of His hand while we recover from the broken journey. That is love.

You may be thinking, "OK, perhaps all of that is true, but there is one thing still missing. What about darkness? God is light. Wouldn't He then just as soon avoid the dark places in which I seek to hide?" It seems to be a logical train of thought, at least at first glance. Scripture tells us that God dwells in unapproachable light. How do we respond to that?

If I say, "Surely the darkness will hide me and the light become night around me," even the darkness will not be dark to you; the night will shine like the day, for darkness is as light to you.

Psalm 139:11-12

Light illuminates the darkness. There is no exception to that rule. Therefore, we can say with confidence that hope, when rightly placed in Jesus, illuminates the darkness both within and around us. We can run and hide, and we can even think we're doing it with good reason. However, there is no place on earth, above it, or under it where we could hide from the Lord, and when His light shines on our darkness, chains break apart and fall to the ground. Lives are healed. Eyes are opened. Captives are set free.

When the Word became flesh and dwelt among us (John 1:14), hope collided with our human existence. For hundreds of years, the people of God had waited and cried out to the Lord, "O Come, O Come Emmanuel, and ransom captive Israel." Then He came, and hope became tangible. His presence brought light to a dark and hopeless world, and His presence that indwells believers to this day by the Holy Spirit continues to shine forth that light into the darkness.

What have we done with the Light that has been entrusted to us? Some have hidden it. Others have risen it. Some have tried to extinguish it, while others have set it ablaze. Some have distorted it, and others have preserved it. The battle between darkness and the Light continues to wage on, and souls are at stake. The darkness looms and threatens the hearts of those who have not embraced the Light.

For each one of us who knows the hope of Jesus, our greatest desire, next to loving the Lord our God with all of our heart, should be loving and leading the lost to His feet. To be without the hope of Christ is to be in spiritual darkness. This is what it means to be spiritually sick. I've known this myself, and I've witnessed it in others. I've been confident of things in my past that simply weren't true. I've been deceived by counterfeit truth. I've also been set free, and it was the Light of Truth that rescued me from the darkness. It was the Light of Jesus Christ that exposed all that festered in my own darkness. His all-consuming light illuminated the darkness in my life and set me free. His light illuminated Kristin's darkness, as well, because hope illuminates.

This is her hope story.

Kristin was raised in captivity. Like an animal caged in a zoo, she was bred in captivity, with only the illusion of freedom. Kristin was 18 months old when her parents joined the "church," and life was never the same.

Both of her parents had been raised in spiritual darkness. They both were searching for something to bring hope, meaning, and purpose to their lives. Drinking, drugs, and partying had provided nothing more than temporary comfort, so when they were first exposed to this "church," they dove in head first. With little to no understanding of the Bible, coupled with years of suffering, mental illness, addiction, and lots of divorce that plagued both sides of their families, this "church" was the first glimmer of perceived hope that they had ever seen. They were young, lost, and grieving—prime targets who were easily deceived—and they latched onto the first thing that offered them any sort of community.

This church is recognized very widely as an underground Christian cult, not as well-known as some others, and it is wrought with legalism. Without an official name, they are referred to as the Two by Twos, or even more commonly and simply called "meeting." Good standing in the church is earned through abiding by a list of dos and don'ts. Everything is completely done in secret. There is no sort of outreach, believing that if someone is desperate enough to really find the truth, that lost person will find them. There is no formal website, no statement of faith, no published legal entity, or anything of the like that might possibly expose them for who they really are. While there is spiritual oversight, it's all very secretive and underground. Everything is hidden.

You can try to approach them on certain doctrines to discuss the issues that are divisive, but there is nothing written, leaving little to no room for debate. There is no assurance of salvation. The strategy of the church is to quiet the questioners, and it's never OK to ask. Even their customized hymnal, which is not allowed to be purchased by "outsiders" or even members without approval of a leader, speaks to this: "Yield unmurmuring obedience, waver not nor turn aside," and "Silence your thoughts and reasonings in subjection to His will." You are simply required to have the faith to accept without seeing. There's no room to explore your faith. There's no room to question.

Because her parents didn't have a foundation in scripture, and therefore lacked any kind of spiritual wisdom and discernment, they accepted everything they were told because they wanted to belong. They raised Kristin to do the same. They essentially divorced their families to enter this new one—nothing more than a counterfeit of truth.

Kristin went from being a very outgoing child with much freedom to dramatic change. Within the course of three weeks, they were completely engulfed in the deception. Some changes were good. Her parents stopped drinking, doing drugs, and partying. They cleaned up their lives in some beautiful ways, but the tragic exchange was the loss of true freedom. This new church became their entire life.

Kristin's first memory of God was hiding under a blanket at age four, desperately trying to hide from a God whom she believed was ashamed of her and incredibly angry with her. At the tender age of four, all she knew of herself was that she was dirty, unclean, and a sinner. Not surprisingly, it was around this time that sexual abuse entered her life from the hands of those within the church. She believed that God hated her. She was terrified by the knowledge that God could see her all the time. The wrath of God was taught and clearly understood, not the love of God, and it wasn't just a wrath against sin, but a vengeful cruelty. This God was not someone she wanted to trust.

Fear drove her to an unrelenting desire to profess, a term the church used which meant to officially join the church and receive salvation. She thought that if she could do this, then maybe, just maybe, she could escape the wrath of hell, a destination toward which she was confident she was heading. The church kept refusing her request, telling her that she wasn't old enough.

At this point in her life, fear was a constant companion. She feared displeasing everyone around her, especially God. She also feared what was required of her in order to gain salvation: standing to her feet in their church meeting and speaking publicly in front of the entire congregation. She was terrified to do that, but she was a gold star addict—wanting to be known as the good girl—and desperate to be seen as one who was doing the right thing.

Trying to rise above her fear, she remained persistent in her pursuit to profess. Once leadership finally relented and gave her permission, to her great disappointment, her parents denied her of this desire, telling her she had to know how to read first in order to take part in the meetings. So, she learned to read that night at six years old, in order to save her soul.

Once she could read, it was then up to her. She was so scared, though, to stand in front of people and speak in public, that it took her two years to gain the courage. On November 2, 1986, a frightened eight-year-old girl stood to her feet and professed, believing that finally she would be saved, hoping that the fear would fade and hope would grow. The next morning, she got up an hour early to read her Bible before school, because now that she was a Christian, she had to do it right. Despite her valiant efforts, the fear remained and grew.

Faith, to her, had become a never-ending game of works. She had to do good to earn salvation and to keep it. She sought this approval in every area of her life. She got good grades in school. She separated herself from the bad kids. She tried to be the perfect child. It was a rat race, and it was exhausting, but she believed in what she was doing. She was just as deceived as her parents were.

When she went to college, she was the only kid from her church who lived in the dorms. Now removed from her comfort zone of religion, she again realized how she had never felt like she belonged with people outside of the church, a lie that had been deeply ingrained into her mind and heart. She still attended meeting three times a week. She believed it all, hook, line, and sinker. She wanted to be all in. She was a pharisee of the pharisees.

The church encouraged people to not be baptized until they were older, when they were more capable of knowing full well what they were doing. As soon as she moved out for college, she wanted to be baptized. Perhaps this next step in an endless game of legalism would finally provide the safety she was desperate for that continued to escape her. To prove her wholehearted devotion, she got baptized in Lake Washington in February. It was cold. Everyone was so excited. Still, what she was looking for didn't come.

Hopes dashed yet again in spite of her many efforts, she gave way to a year's worth of rebellion, which was so unlike her. She fell in love with a boy who wasn't a part of the church, started partying with him, slept with him, and began to live a double life. She would go to church and look holy, and then go back to college to quickly return to her life of sin. It was exhilarating and terrifying at the same time. She was hiding it, something that the church had inadvertently taught her to do well.

There was a guilt that finally caught up to her and brought her back to confession. She felt she had penance to do in order to make herself clean again. She sought answers from the leaders of the church on what she could do to make it right, but they had none. Once her story was known within the church, the gossip was humiliating, and she walked in shame into every church gathering. Still, she did what she knew best. The good girl returned. The strategy was so exhausting.

It's very interesting to her that in a church that teaches there really is no forgiveness, only the need to live a perfect life, many of the people in the church seemed very content to lead double lives. Everything looked perfect, but nothing felt right. Look good on the outside. Do whatever you want. Don't get caught. She struggled to reconcile it all. Pious, outward lives were somehow merged with private, inner lives that didn't even come close to matching the outward expression. Since she couldn't make sense of it, she simply chose to blend into it.

She met the man who would become her husband when she was 23, and it was a speedy romance. They dated six weeks and got engaged. She finally thought she had found someone to love her like her dad loved her mom. He was 12 years older than her, charming, and mysterious. She was swept off her feet. Being courted by him was probably the highlight of her life up until that time. She knew little about him, but she had met him in the church, so she assumed there was no cause for concern. People tried to warn her, but she was blinded by infatuation.

Ignoring all the warning signs, they were married a short time later, only for her to realize that he also lived two separate lives. What could she do but accept it? That's all she saw in everyone around her, so why not in her husband, too? They partied together, and then went to church hungover the next day. As stress and anxiety grew within her, she grew uncomfortable at the thought of her two worlds colliding.

Still, she believed that this church was the only way, and if she did better, she could find hope. They had their first child, a miracle she thought she would never be able to know, and then nothing short of disaster erupted in their lives. Death in the family, loss of a job and a home, addictions, and so much more threatened their family. She remembers holding her little son and thinking, "What am I going to tell him about God?" Her husband had become very depressed, and he found his comfort in ways that only brought more darkness into their home, an ever-increasing darkness that seemed to engulf her.

They went to marriage counseling because she was at a breaking point. Through counseling, very much unexpectedly, she gained the courage to express her desire to check out other churches in the area. Her husband was desperate enough to say yes because he wanted to stay married. Divorce was a fate almost worse than death in the church, since they teach that divorce and remarriage are not permitted under any circumstances.

For months, she sat on this newfound freedom, afraid to explore the possibility that she might have been wrong all along. The confusion within her grew, and the questions began to stir. Still, she couldn't seem to fully shake the deception because it was all she had ever known. Now pregnant with their second child and still searching for a new church, she reached out to some old friends who had left the church years prior to pursue Jesus, and they helped point her in the right direction.

The first church she went to was a Christian church with drip coffee, an acoustic guitar, and a small, hand-held drum. People were dressed casually, and she thought it was so irreverent to be so informal. Someone said "Hallelujah" in the middle of the prayer, and for the first time, she saw people's hands raised in worship. She freaked out, and she didn't try any new churches for a year. She had swallowed the pill of the cult, and the deep, legalistic programming within her was proving to be incredibly difficult to uproot.

Becoming a mom had caused her to start asking questions, though. Light began to shine. It had once sounded so beautiful to her to hear the words of their hymns sung aloud in meeting, the songs she had been singing her entire life, but now she heard fear and judgment in those lyrics. She was unable to sit comfortably through meetings anymore. The place where she had always felt she belonged the most was becoming the place she feared the most.

She still didn't know who Jesus was. She didn't know what to believe. At one home meeting, several of her close friends had stood up to give their testimonies, and they all said how grateful they were that they weren't like those other people in the "false" Christian churches. A light bulb went on in her mind. It was a tangible illumination to her when she realized that they, in fact, were the pharisees. They were congratulating themselves on their own righteousness, not grieving for those who were lost.

The questions that she had tried to hold in up until this point kept finding their way out of her mouth. "If we really are the only way, the only right church, then why aren't we reaching out to the lost? Where is our heart for the lost?" They had no answers that could satisfy the holy discontent within her, and it didn't stop there. More things within the church became an uncomfortable rub to her. Once she had seen her dissatisfaction, she couldn't go back. The very people to whom she had belonged for so long no longer felt safe to her.

She was alone and scared. She couldn't take her concerns about her marriage to the leaders in the church. So, she went to God, and she prayed the first, bold prayer of her life. "If it's in the Bible, I want to believe it. If it's not, I don't want it." She invited God to transform her mind. The people in the church warned her against that, encouraging her to just obey what they said, but she could no longer trust their voices. As light began to shine in and the deception was slowly being uncovered, she stood up in church and spoke boldly and honestly about all that she was now experiencing. One week later, she received a corrective letter from a minister in Australia telling her that she was on a dangerous road.

She didn't care anymore. The weight of false religion was a burden too heavy for her to bear, and she was desperate for truth. She gained courage to start looking at other churches again, and found one where she stayed for five years. She heard the doctrine of the Incarnation of Jesus Christ and the Trinity, and that revelation tore her dearly-held false beliefs from top to bottom. It was upon this foundation that she found Jesus Christ, and it was the perfect place for her to be birthed in Christ. Weekly, she received in-depth Bible teaching, and through that, she began to understand the Bible in context.

To know that Jesus is God illuminated everything within her. It set her free. For the first time in her life, she finally felt safe. There had always been so much fear of God because she never really knew who He was. Now that she knew Jesus was God and that Jesus was her intercessor, it changed everything. There was no turning back for her.

She told her husband that she wasn't going to go back to the cult. He said it was as bad as if she had told him she was diagnosed with terminal cancer. The news was just as devastating to their family. She could no longer accept living in mediocre Christianity, having a form of godliness but denying its power. She could no longer accept this "other gospel" that denied the deity of Christ. For the first time, she didn't care about breaking the rules. She had finally found hope, and it was in Jesus.

This departure made her infamous in the church. It was scandalous to leave for becoming a Christian. All other reasons for leaving were far more understandable than to leave for loving Jesus. This was the ultimate betrayal. She didn't care. She had Jesus.

She waited, holding her breath for years for her husband to walk in the door and get saved. She sobbed through church, desiring this more than anything. So much time in her life had been wasted in deception and darkness, and all she wanted now was the salvation of her family, but it didn't come. In the waiting, she learned to believe that Jesus really did love her. She started singing it to her kids. She taught her little boy how to say "Hallelujah."

The joy she now knew did not remove the sorrow. This was simultaneously a season of death and a season of new life. She lost all of her friends. She was cut off from everything she had ever known. She had to relearn everything—how to dress, how to sing, how to read the Bible— but the new life came through the Word of God. She couldn't get enough of Jesus and God's Word. She started to devour the Bible, reading it 10-15 hours a week. She listened to sermons and podcasts. She was starved for truth.

Now, nine years later and despite her longing for her children and husband to know the hope she now has, she no longer lives in fear. She knows that if God can save her, He can save anyone. His light is able to illuminate any darkness, even the darkness that lived inside of her. Jesus plus nothing equals everything. It's just Jesus. That is the hope to which she clings. It's easier to have a list of what you should do than to accept the free gift of grace. Maybe that's why it took her so long to get there, but in the end, she couldn't escape His call.

That's where she lives now, in the light of His truth. Just within the last few months, God finally set her free from her marriage. She did everything she could, believing that the end of her story would be her husband's salvation. She begged God, she promised God, and she bargained with God. She even offered her own life if it would mean her family coming to know the Lord. She prayed for the grace of God to ambush him like it had for her. It still hasn't come. Even so, her hope remains in Jesus. He is the treasure hidden in the field, and He is worth everything she left behind.

God is still stripping away the last bits of her bent toward religion, and there are days when she struggles to believe that God's forgiveness will cover this, too. However, her story isn't finished being written. God will complete the good work He started in her. Light continues to shine into every part of the darkness. Life isn't easy, and it certainly isn't free from pain, but it is filled with light, and now she can finally see. Seeing is everything, because she can now walk in the light and help usher others into the light—the light that she now knows, the light that has set her free. He has proven Himself to be her Provider. She is not just walking in His permission, but she is also walking in His favor.

She takes great comfort now in knowing that God sees her all of the time. His eye is on the sparrow, so she builds her nest and raises her young at His feet. He knows the hairs on her head. He rejoices over her with singing. He pays attention to the details. Therefore, she has hope for the future. Hope illuminates.

CHAPTER 8

HOPE REBUILDS

ALL YOU CAN see is brokenness. All that appears to remain are the ashes of what once was. Everything is shattered. All seems lost. Life is mere wreckage. The present is filled with dread, and the future holds nothing but fear. Where is hope to be found now?

This one is for you, the one who has named herself "Unworthy." To the one who wears the brand "Broken"—these words are for you, written to you. To the captive, the prisoner, the one bound by insecurity and hopelessness: This message was written with you in mind. May these words dig deeper than the pain you carry, and may these words plant seeds of hope—a hope to rebuild the life that has been broken down, a hope to restore the places long devastated, a hope to bring life to what seems lifeless, and a hope to renew your mind.

I find that there is no better place to begin the rebuilding than with the Rebuilder Himself and with His own words. His words, far more than the best words any human could ever offer, are healing balm to our bleeding wounds. His words give the life and hope for which our hearts are desperate. His words rebuild. His words bring life to the dust and beauty from the ashes.

> *The Spirit of the Sovereign Lord is on me, because the Lord has anointed me to proclaim good news to the poor. He has sent me to bind up the brokenhearted, to proclaim freedom for the captives and release from darkness for the prisoners,*
>
> *to proclaim the year of the Lord's favor and the day of vengeance of our God, to comfort all who mourn,*
>
> *and provide for those who grieve in Zion—to bestow on them a crown of beauty instead of ashes, the oil of joy instead of mourning, and a garment of praise instead of a spirit of despair.*
>
> *They will be called oaks of righteousness, a planting of the Lord for the display of his splendor.*
>
> Isaiah 61:1-3

Hope begins to be uncovered and found at the reading of His Word. When we look to the Truth, we find truth.

When we look to Hope, we find hope. When we let the light shine into our darkness, healing can begin. When we start to see Him for who He really is, hope becomes our home.

In just three short verses of Scripture, we have a beautifully accurate description of the work of Jesus Christ. He came to proclaim good news. His message was intended for the poor. His mission was to bind up, or heal, brokenhearted people. His work effectively sets the captives free. He offered to exchange our darkness for His light to all who remained imprisoned in darkness. He brought with Him the favor of God in one hand and the justice of God in the other. He came to comfort those who mourn and to catch every tear of those who grieve. He brought beauty for the one who was covered in ashes and joy for the one who was clothed in despair. With Him came a new Kingdom—one that would establish hope in the hearts of its people, one that would bear the fruit of righteousness to trample out all wickedness.

These verses pour forth one beautiful description after another of the redeeming, rebuilding, renewing, and restoring work of Jesus Christ. These words come packed with power and strength. These words deposit hope into hopeless hearts, a hope to believe that all is not lost in Christ, but rather, all is made new. He alone is able to make beautiful things out of the dust of our broken lives. He alone is able to bring freedom to the one who has only known bondage. He alone is able to provide joy and gladness for the weary heart who has long since forgotten what it means to rejoice and sing. He alone is able.

I've spent the past fifteen plus years of my life believing these next few words with all that I am:

It is absolutely critical to not only know what you believe, but you must know why you believe what you believe.

Many will say that they believe in God or at least some form of a higher power concept, but if pressed a bit further, I wonder how many of those same people would be able to give a reason as to why. Can you defend the faith to which you hold? Can I?

It was in my college years that I began to study the attributes of God, or in other words, the character of God. For almost a year, I sat under the teaching and instruction of a beloved mentor in my life as she walked me through Scripture. If you search through the Bible, you will find many defining characteristics of who God says He is: Faithful, Just, Holy, Good, Righteous, Sovereign, Immutable, Omnipotent, Omnipresent, Omniscient, Loving, Merciful, and Forgiving, just to name a few.

The moment I began to uncover His character, the deeper my faith in Him grew. To know about God is an ocean apart from actually knowing God. For example, I can pick my celebrity of choice and find countless facts, details, and pieces of information about them by simply searching on the internet. Do I really know them, though? Well, here's the funny thing. Through that research, I can easily trick myself into thinking that I do. Am I right? How many of you have done the same? We do this with social media, too. It could be years since we last saw someone or even talked to them, but it feels like days, maybe less, because we've followed their play by play on Facebook or Instagram. It's a false sense of knowledge. It's the appearance of something that isn't actually so.

I have found this method to be true in my relationship with God. From the time I was a young child, I was told many things about God. I sat through church and Sunday school for years. I read the Bible stories. I memorized the verses. By the age of five, I could tell a perfect stranger about Jesus and invite them to be saved. I had much knowledge about God.

It wasn't until my early adult years, though, that I began to get to know God for myself. Many well-intended people had fed to me their thoughts on God, and my faith had become a collage of all of that passed along information. However, until I discovered for myself who God says He is in His Word, I was unable to give an adequate answer to this question: "Do you know why you believe what you believe?" I could no longer ride the waves of my mom's faith or my pastor's faith. My faith had to become my own, and when it did, everything changed. It brought hope.

Many things in this life inform us of who God is and dictate our own beliefs about Him. Whether it's the teaching we received in the various churches we attended growing up, or perhaps, and maybe even more importantly, the circumstances we endured throughout our lives, our understanding of who God is can often be shaped by everything else but His Word. We reach adulthood with a lifetime of both traumas and triumphs, and we blend all of it together with shreds of truth here and there, and out comes a theological smoothie of incredibly inaccurate proportions. We allow what we have experienced to inform us about God, instead of allowing His own Word to do that work.

It seems only natural to conclude that our experiences are the best way to arrive at an understanding of God, but I'm going to submit to you a better way. People will falsify truth, and circumstances will lie to us. Our own emotional responses to these things will add to that confusion, so we must learn that those things are not the foundation upon which we want to build our belief systems. They crumble over time, and they will inevitably fall, but our God will do neither. We must learn to drag our brokenness into the light of His Word, and we must learn to allow its truth to rewire our minds with hope.

So, who is God? What does He say about Himself in His Word? How does He reveal Himself and His works to us? Who can we know Him to be in His Word? Looking at only Isaiah 61:1-3, let's start with this:

God is our Provider.

The person who has lived with lack needs to know this truth about our God. He brings good news to the poor. He meets the needs of the needy with Himself. The good news is the hope of salvation. Without it, we would have nothing to live for. God, seeing the brokenness of mankind, left His heavenly throne, and came to us in this broken world and in our broken condition, to bring us the good news of hope beyond this hard life—a hope to be had and known in His Son, Jesus Christ. That is provision at its best. It's generosity at its finest. It's a life of abundance that we could not attain, but God chose to generously provide for those who would receive His Son.

God is our Healer.

To the one who eagerly awaits the healing so desperately needed in their life, this truth is for you. Every wound you have endured on this side of heaven, every sorrow, every hurt, every pain—our God is able to heal. He is the Great

Physician of our hearts. He is the creator of life, and He is the sustainer of life. He came for the express purpose to bind up the wounds of the brokenhearted. He came so that we no longer had to be defined by our brokenness and suffering, but instead, we could be known as whole. He sees the injustice that is inflicted upon His children, and He rises to heal the hurt. He moved from His seat in Heaven to bend down into the pain of this earth, and He took that pain upon Himself. Through His life, death, and resurrection, He lives to make all things new.

God is our Redeemer.

It was our own sin that caused us to be pit-dwellers, but God reached down into those very pits that we dug, and He drew us up and out of them. He sets the prisoner free. He rescues the addict, the depressed, the doubter, the fearful, the victim, the abused, the wayward, and the lowly, and He releases them from the darkness that binds them in captivity. He is the God of freedom, and freedom is the known and experienced reality for all who seek Him first. He redeems broken stories to make them beautiful. He delivers us from the death sentence that our sin would lead us to. He is Redeemer.

God is our Justice.

We live in a world that so often fails to uphold justice for the innocent, but our God never fails in this regard.

We rage and roar with anger in disbelief as we watch injustice go unpunished, but our God sees all. Nothing escapes His watchful eye. He is just, and one day, He will set all things right. The victim will stand in victory over the victimizer. The marginalized and the outcast will be welcomed and wanted in Him. His Word speaks louder than our circumstances ever could. Hope can be found on the pages of His truth. This is our God.

God is our Comfort.

To those whose only companion seems to be your tears, this truth is for you. The weary and grieving heart can find comfort in His presence. His love and mercy invites us to weep against His chest, to be held in His arms, and to know safety in His embrace. We can bring our hurts, disappointments, fears, and losses to His hands, because His hands will always be big enough to carry them; and while our circumstances might not change, our perspective of them will in His presence. He comforts those who mourn. He comforts our grief like nothing else can. This is beauty from ashes. This is our God.

God is our Rebuilder.

To know Him is to know the hope that rebuilds. Because He makes all things new and because He works all things out for good, we can be confident that He is performing that same redemptive work in our pain. The divine exchange of our ashes for His beauty astounds me. He takes our mourning and turns it into joy. He replaces our garments of despair with a covering of praise. He rebuilds the brokenness of our lives. This hope rebuilds the places that have been long devastated—the ruins of our hearts, the shambles of our pasts, the bleakness of our present—and it replaces the fear of our future with a hope for eternity.

This is our God. Knowing Him changes everything. The journey of knowing Him effectively rewrites the painful stories of our yesterdays and gives us hope for our tomorrows. Isaiah 61 is a passage, among many, which speaks to the unchanging character of our God, a character that remains the same even when our circumstances don't. The hope we are after today far surpasses the wishing that perhaps one day things will get easier. A wish that someday, things might get better, isn't hope at all.

Hope is strong. Hope is confident. Hope is unwavering. Hope trusts and believes, because hope, true hope, is in Jesus Christ. This is the hope that rebuilds all things needing restoration. This hope allows our brokenness to become opportunity. This hope opens our eyes to see all that God has in store for those He loves.

As doubt seeks to creep in and plague your mind once

again to believe that your ashes could never be beauty and that your pain could never have a holy purpose, allow me to invite you to take one step further into the conversation of "hope rebuilds." Hear the words of another, someone who has been in the deepest, darkest depths, and is now beginning to see that hope is rebuilding the ashes of her life, turning them into something far more beautiful than she can yet see. Sue's story of hope will be so worth the read.

This is her hope story.

I remember the day I met sweet Sue. She sat toward the front of my Bible study class, as close as her fear would allow her to go, and just far enough away to make her feel safe. This was new territory for her. These were uncharted waters. She had never taken a Bible study before. Her limited understanding of God had been tainted by grief, pain, and trauma that are simply unimaginable.

Abuse in every possible form came charging into her life at the young and tender age of three. The sound of her father's footsteps coming down the hall toward her bedroom in the middle of the night haunts her dreams. The perverse actions said to be done in the name of love forced her to escape to places other than the present in order to survive the trauma and the ongoing abuse. "Don't make a sound," he would say each night as he came in to rob her of her innocence, and so she learned to hate breathing.

To only ever know wrong and evil, forces one to struggle with the ability to accept and embrace what is right. When the physical abuse started to come from her brother, she only knew to believe that she deserved it. She lived in constant terror and fear, and her only mechanism of survival was to escape in her mind, to go to places where the abuse was not happening. She created another world inside of herself, and as the trauma continued to increase in frequency, a once whole child became a very fragmented soul.

There was only confusion surrounding the conversation of God. Her family wore their church hats on Sundays and were well-respected in their community, but there was nothing but darkness and evil that existed behind closed doors. Ties to Free Masonry filled her family's legacy, and the effects of that were known, felt, and experienced within the walls of their home. How could she understand God to be anything but unloving, vengeful, and full of wrath?

The only communication she ever received from her dad was abuse that was twisted with words of love. She never heard "I love you" from her mom, but her dad would say it often. Her mother made it clear that she never wanted her, and her brother often tried to kill her.

Life was a nightmare, but not even sleep provided an escape from it.

She learned to live hardened by all of the abuse she was forced to endure. Her circumstances shouted a false identity at her that she only knew to accept as true—that she was dirty, violated, unworthy, and unlovable. So, she began to live that way. She knew that no one truly loved her, and that knowledge had taught her to not love herself. She loathed herself but masked it with rebellion. She learned ways to behave, when necessary, that would keep the attention off of her, but she could not escape the pain that violently roared inside of her soul.

There are defining moments in our lives that shape who we are, whether we desire them to or not. Sue has had many of these. There was the time when the abuse was finally brought to light and held up for all to see in the legal system, only to result in her mother refusing to believe that it was true and choosing her father over her. Hopes dashed. The lies of "worthless" and "unlovable" continued to scream at the top of their lungs. Then, there was that night, that one fateful night, when the stranger chose to take advantage of her inability to restrain him, and he took whatever innocence she might have had left. With hope against hope, she mustered up every ounce of courage she could find within herself and took him to court with the accusation of rape, only to be told by the judge that it was her fault. She shouldn't have had that one drink that night.

She learned to bury the pain, because dealing with it was impossible and far too painful. Nothing made sense if she tried to work through it, so she didn't bother, and twenty years of trying to sweep things under the rug found her to be not much more than a shell of a person— lifeless and hopeless. Twenty years of marriage and seven children later, Sue found her purpose in raising her littles to know love, support, and comfort from her arms—things she had never been afforded. She was determined to provide for them the safety and security that she had never known. Serving as a distraction from the pain of her own life, she poured herself into her children. She reserved nothing for herself. While just about every one of her needs went unmet, she made sure their's were met.

When life's events finally moved her from the town of her childhood across the country to the desert of Arizona, she decided that it was time to invest a bit more into herself. Finding a good church, unlike the one in which she had been raised, was of utmost priority. Weekly attendance led to an increased desire for more of Jesus, and as she began to turn to Jesus more and more, her husband turned away from Him, more and more. Her newfound faith in Christ was constantly demeaned and downplayed in her home, and the struggle intensified within her. For the first time in her entire life, she was beginning to taste something she had never been exposed to before: Hope. She was desperate for more, but she was being forced to pursue it alone.

The wedge in her marriage only continued to grow, and the gap between them, which once seemed small, was miles apart. Trust was evaporating, and apart from her children, home no longer felt like a safe place to be. She was desperately trying to cling to Jesus, a new concept for her, but the circumstances of her life, coupled with the horrors from her past that she was trying to work through in therapy, kept trying to beat her down.

Some days were better than others. Some days were much worse. When the darkness of her past would take over, self-harm would erupt. She would awake with terror, only to find marks and bruises on her body, unaware of how they got there. She would run to the Bible, soaking up every truth, eager to transform the way her mind perceived things, and then find herself spiraling out of control. It was the worst roller coaster ride imaginable, and it was taking its toll on her.

Her marriage continued to deteriorate as her faith in Jesus continued to grow. When the divorce was finalized, she was now forced into deeper waters than she had ever thought possible to endure. Now, a single mom with little income, in need of a place to call home, her faith was called into action to navigate these deep waters.

Through the love and support of a faithful group of family and friends around her, she was able to find a safe home for herself and her children, a place where stories could be rewritten and hope could be rebuilt.

Horrific memories continue to plague her mind to this day. Flashbacks and night terrors fill her days and nights with dread and fear. Realizations of a life of trauma and abuse that she had suppressed seek to overcome her as she fights for freedom, healing, and new life every single day. There isn't a day that goes by without a fight to survive, but the one thing that has begun to change it all is that she now knows the love of Jesus, even if only in part. She has seen the light of Jesus come into her broken story, and she has witnessed Him beginning to rebuild all that has been broken.

I have never known someone with as much resolve to keep going as Sue. She never gives up, even when all the odds seem to be stacked entirely against her. God keeps showing up, being faithful, and seeing her safely through. Her children, who were raised in a spiritually divided home, are now one by one making personal decisions for Jesus. Her fight has been excruciating, long, and ever so hard, but she keeps fighting the good fight of faith. She keeps clinging to the hope she now has with everything left inside of her.

There are many days when she falls hard to the ground

and is once again bound by fear. There are days when the terror takes over, and she visibly shakes in fear. There are days when the lies shout much louder than the truth inside her head. There are days when she forgets whom to trust and what to believe. It is in those times that we rush to her side, graciously and lovingly pulling her back to the arms of Jesus. It is the same grace each one of us has received from Him ourselves, so we continue to give it out generously to her.

As I sit here capturing the details of her story into words, tears stream down my face. I love this woman. She is family to me. She is "Auntie" to my son. To know Sue is to experience joy. I refer to her as sweet Sue because she is nothing but sweet and kind in a world that has dealt her nothing but hell. I would never wish even a fraction of this amount of trauma on my worst enemy, and yet she has endured what I have captured and so much more. I ache and long for her full healing in Jesus. I am so desirous for her to be made completely whole inside. I know the hope of Jesus that is able to rebuild all things broken and destroyed. Every day, I see glimpses of this rebuilding in her life, and I continue on in hope that one day, she will be whole and complete, lacking nothing, and full of joy and praise.

Hope rebuilds, sometimes one, slow step at a time. It reaches into the broken, shattered pieces of our lives, and it pieces them back together to create something far more beautiful than the original work. Hope replaces the ashes of our pain with a beautiful headdress to mark us with radiant light. Hope takes the despair and grief, and builds joy and praise in their place. Hope has done this in Sue's heart, and it will continue to until the work is complete.

> *...being confident of this, that He who began a good work in you will carry it on to completion until the day of Christ Jesus.*
>
> **Philippians 1:6**

CHAPTER 9

HOPE RISES

Let not the flood sweep over me,
or the deep swallow me up,
or the pit close its mouth over me.

Psalm 69:15

HAVE YOU EVER been there? Has life ever felt like a never-ending battle to stay afloat, treading water, trying to keep your head above the waves? Have you spent any time in the depths of despair? Do you understand the constant dread of an uphill fight, the fight to get out of the pit that has held you for so long?

You are so welcome here, today, my friend. You are in good company. The desperation that bleeds through the words of Psalm 69 is all too common for so many of us. Life hurts. The pain is real. Darkness overwhelms. No human being is immune to it. King David, the writer of Psalm 69, knew all of this well.

I think it's easy for us to attribute superhuman ability and strength to the men and women we read about in the

Bible. I mean, a guy who couldn't speak well (Moses) petitioned a pharaoh (the most powerful man on earth at the time) numerous times to "Let my people go," and he actually won that war of words. What about that guy (Noah) who saved a remnant of mankind and animals on an ark of massive proportions that he built with his own hands to withstand a flood that would wipe out every other living thing? Don't forget that one lady (Sarah) who became a mom in her nineties, and through that child, became the mother to a nation that would outnumber the stars. Of course, there are many others that could be mentioned: Elijah who was caught up to Heaven on a chariot, Rahab the prostitute who played a key role in saving the people of God, Mary who gave birth to Jesus, Peter who walked on water, and the list could go on and on.

If we only play the highlight reel of our heroes of the faith, we will fail to remember that they were painfully human, too. They had fallen and imperfect stories, and the blood running through their veins was just as human as ours. They messed up. They failed daily. They struggled at times to believe and to hope. They needed grace, mercy, and forgiveness every single day of their lives. They had faith, yes, and it was their faith that was a catalyst in connecting their lives to the powerful story of Jesus, just like you and me. Still, they knew well what the walls of the pit looked like, because all of them had spent their fair share of time in one pit or another.

If there was ever a writer in Scripture that captured so beautifully the tension between hope and despair, it was King David. Throughout the Psalms that he wrote, his internal struggle between doubt and faith, between fear and courage, between angst and praise, and between despair and hope is nearly palpable. Perhaps, that is why the Psalms are so beloved by so many, because they are so real. They are authentic. They are genuine. They are vulnerable, and they portray the good, the bad, and the ugly.

We need this kind of authenticity to come alive in the church today. If God saw fit that this type of honest conversation surrounding pain would be included in the Bible, then we can assume that He intended for the conversation to continue today. Too many hurting and struggling people find it difficult to call church "home" when their pain and suffering feels so minimalized. When we don't talk about despair and depression within the walls of the church, those who suffer from it feel as if their pain does not belong. We could not be further from the heart of God if we are not rushing toward hurting people. It's just who He is, and it's who He desires us to be.

It's easy for us to frequent the promises of God in Scripture, isn't it? It's natural for us to open up our Bibles and to search for words that will bring joy and hope, but how often do we wrestle with the tension of pain? Do we understand that it is a tension? God is good yet people suffer. There is much tension in that. It's a hard and messy and difficult conversation to navigate. So, what have we done? Well, some have engaged in the mess of the pain. We wouldn't be where we are today if they hadn't. Still, many have avoided it.

God's Word leans into the tension of pain, though. God's Word engages in the dialogue. God's Word gives room to have the conversation, and King David's voice is one of the loudest in this tension.

Just take a look at Psalm 69. The opening twelve verses are David's laments. He mourns. He grieves. He openly expresses his dissatisfaction about his circumstances to God. He does not hold back. Why should he? He knows that God can handle it. He has spent enough time in the presence of God to know and understand who He is, and so he brings it all to Him, time and time again.

> *I am weary with my crying out; my throat is parched. My eyes grow dim with waiting for my God.*
>
> **Psalm 69:3**

I know that place. Do you? I have been there. I imagine you have, too. I have cried more tears than I thought existed inside of me. I have run out of words and the energy to pray them in times of my own despair. I have lost sight of the greater purpose in seasons of my own pain. I've grown tired and weary in times of waiting on the Lord, waiting for Him to act and to move on my behalf. Allow me to give you permission today to admit the same. If we're honest, I bet we all have been there. So, let's lean into it together.

David knew this, too. He knew the pain of hurt, disappointment, sorrow, and loss. He was personally acquainted with the depths of despair. He knew what it felt like to have no one to turn to. He had personally experienced the bitter sting of betrayal. He knew what it meant to fear for his very life. He lived in the pain of waiting on God to fulfill promises.

He also knew his God. He knew the God who welcomes both the praises and the desperate cries of His people. So, David brought both. He brought the sorrow, and he brought the song. He brought the lament, and he brought the praise. Pain and suffering beautifully collide with faith and hope in his inspired words. Twelve verses of despair, anguish, desperation, and weariness are followed by a refrain of prayer, hope, trust, praise, and faith.

> *But as for me, my prayer is to you, O Lord. At an acceptable time, O God, in the abundance of your steadfast love*

answer me in your saving faithfulness.

Deliver me from sinking in the mire; let me be delivered from my enemies and from the deep waters.

Let not the flood sweep over me, or the deep swallow me up, or the pit close its mouth over me.

Answer me, O Lord, for your steadfast love is good; according to your abundant mercy, turn to me.

Psalm 69:13-16

In the middle of his pain, he makes a choice to return to hope. When his own clock has run out of time for things to change, he trusts in God's perfect timing to rescue him. He chooses to not forget who God is. He doesn't stop asking God for that which he wants. He still prays for deliverance. He still asks for God to save Him. He still desires to be rescued, but while he waits for those things to come, he chooses to remember that hope rises. Hope rises from the pit, because hope is in a person and not in a destination. He knows that choosing hope won't necessarily change the immediate details of his circumstance, but he knows it will change how he sees them.

Allow me to submit something to you today that might surprise you. A good, long, hard look at the darkness causes the light to appear that much brighter. What am I suggesting to you? Perhaps, it would benefit us to sit in the pain, to look at the darkness of despair, to take time to wrestle with it for long enough so that when the light of Christ shines in, it will be that much more attractive to us. Instead of slinging Christian platitudes at one another in times of our deepest pain and suffering, what if we mourned with those who mourned? What if providing space for the pain to be fleshed out and truly felt actually invited the light to come in? What if this is exactly what God wanted us to do all along?

David knew this to be true. He allowed himself time to sit in the places of his hurt, and he gave himself permission to bring his grievances before the Lord, knowing that every time, he would find a receptive audience in God. David penned some of the most beautiful words in Scripture, and it wasn't just the Psalms of praise that he wrote that fall into that category. It was his brutal honesty and complete vulnerability that invite us into the depths of relationship with God like David knew.

How else do you think David inherited the title "A man after God's own heart?" Despite what came his way, he determined himself to be found in God. In the good times, he danced before the Lord. In the bad times, he wept before the Lord. Notice, though, that in all times, he was putting himself before the Lord.

That is where hope is found. It is not found in self-sufficiency or in the false assumption that God is too busy for this burden that you're currently carrying. It is not found in isolation, in pushing God and others away because it seems easier to be alone in your pain. Hope is found in the pursuit of Jesus Christ, our King, and it's found in both the good and the bad days of our lives. Hope can be had and fully known on the mountain top and in the deepest valley. Where are we looking for it?

Are you willing to go there? Are you willing to be honest about your pain before the Lord? I'm not asking if you're willing to talk about your pain. Many of us are. The problem is not being willing to talk about it, but rather, being willing to bring it to the Lord. Often, we will take our pain to everyone but Him. We spill out our hurt, discouragement, and disappointment onto others. Is that necessarily bad? No, it's not, as long as we've taken it to God first. God created community, so of course, He desires that we be in community with others. It's simply a matter of priorities. God comes first. People come second. The problem with reversing the order is that people weren't intended to handle our pain. We don't know how to carry it well. It weighs us down. The weight of our pain was always intended to be shouldered by Jesus first. Call Him first. Phone a friend second.

No amount of sorrow, hurt, betrayal, or pain is too much for our God to bear. He can handle it. He did handle it on the cross. So, take yours to Him. Trust Him with the wounds of your story. Find Him in the words of the psalmists who cried out in desperation for God to meet them in their pain. True hope rises from the pits of our despair to acknowledge that our God remains the Solid Rock upon which we can stand. All else might be shaken and moved, but our God is not.

The same David who wrote the words of heartache and despair in Psalm 69 also penned these words of hope:

> *O LORD my God, I cried to you for help, and you have healed me. O LORD, you have brought up my soul from Sheol; you restored me to life from among those who go down to the pit.*

Psalm 30:2-3

> *He drew me up from the pit of destruction, out of the miry bog, and set my feet upon a rock, making my steps secure.*

Psalm 40:2

*Bless the Lord, O my soul, and all that
is within me, bless his holy name! Bless
the Lord, O my soul, and forget not
all his benefits, who forgives all your
iniquity, who heals all your diseases,
who redeems your life from the pit,
who crowns you with steadfast love
and mercy, who satisfies you with good
so that your youth is renewed like the
eagle's.*

Psalm 103:1-5

The beauty in reading these passages from Psalms together is that it gives us permission to know, feel, and experience both sides of the coin in our relationship with God. We will have dark days, and we can mourn and grieve those times. We will also find hope in God and experience His healing and our prayers being answered, and we can rejoice in that and celebrate those times. The Psalms give space for both the sorrow and the song. Do you see that? We are welcomed into the story of the faithful who have gone before us, and we are shown how to walk just as faithfully as they did.

The pits of despair and the darkness of depression are not the end of our story in Christ. Despite the place in which we find ourselves today, we have this hope, this anchor for our souls, and this hope changes everything.

This hope raises us up out of our pits, refusing to allow those dark places to be our final destination. This hope lifts up our heads from the muck and the mire of our pain, and it fixes our eyes back on Jesus. This hope whispers in our joy and shouts in our pain, constantly bringing us back to our never-ending need for Jesus. Hope rises.

This is her hope story.

Deafening loneliness, hopeless despair, dark depression—all places Taylor has known well. Even while immersed in environments of faith, the darkness lingered and threatened a life of hopelessness and defeat. Would she ever know anything else, any other reality?

Depression has always been a part of her story. Although unable to define it as such when she was young, there has been a consistent thread, a deep sense of loneliness that has seemed to follow her through this life. To give voice to her pain through sharing about her struggle seemed impossible, so she chalked it up to typical teenage angst and forced herself to keep going, smiling on the outside but aching within herself. How could she excuse these feelings of despair when her life looked so good from a distance?

As many of us know well, outward appearances are not always accurate reflections of what is going on inside.

To the world, Taylor was the poster child of success. She was the student body president, captain of the dance team, a cheerleader on the varsity squad, and a "known" face by nearly everyone in school, but none of that mattered. Despite this perfect girl image that everyone else saw, she had never felt so alone.

It made little sense even to her. Why did she feel this way? Where was her joy? She couldn't reconcile her good life with her dark emotions, but little did she know that depression is no respecter of persons, and it does not discriminate. So, she kept going, kept faking, kept trying to please everyone around her, determined to mask her pain with activity.

Unexpected tragedy has a way of revealing our true colors, forcing out what resides deep inside the recesses of our hearts. When her younger brother, Chase, died suddenly in his sleep one night, the darkness settled all around her. Up until that point in her life, she was able to keep going and outshine the despair within her, but that fight was now gone. Her new, daily reality became depression. She knew now what to call it, but she had no idea how to overcome it.

Perhaps a new life and a fresh, clean slate at college would be the long, awaited prescription to heal her pain. Maybe she could find purpose and hope in this life there, creating a new image with new friends, a life that she could rewrite to a new tune. Despite her valiant efforts, the downward spiral only increased in its intensity. A young woman who had once been so convinced of her beliefs and values suddenly found herself compromising the very things upon which she had staked her life. As her moral compass veered further from the once very clear path, the more lost she felt in the haze of it all.

By this point, she had taught herself to live for the approval of others. How other people perceived her, even those who didn't know her well, meant everything to her. She rose and fell on the words of others and what they had to say about her. Well, words can cut like a knife. They can damage our hearts in ways that seem irreparable. When these damaging words came from the most trusted friend in Taylor's life, she found herself in the deepest pit, the darkest place she could have ever imagined.

Aside from calling herself a Christian, God was no longer an active part of her life. Feeling distanced from God, coupled with the pain of relational loss, there was no joy to be found in her. Nothing made her happy anymore. She had mastered the art of pretending, but the ache inside was becoming increasingly more difficult to cover up. So much energy was required to just exist. Interactions with people were exhausting and painful. She felt so alone.

Even in her attempts to run from God and push Him away, God was still pursuing her. Jason had been in her life since her freshman year, and it was this relationship that would prove to be the catalyst in her return to the Lord. They began to seek after God together, and as their faith continued to grow, she began to experience true hope and see light on the horizon for the first time in her life. What had at one time seemed like an endless, dark road was beginning to emerge into something so beautiful, something with glimmers of hope. The depression didn't evaporate, but the light became brighter as the darkness faded.

The seasons of life that would follow came with waves of the sadness and loneliness of her past, but they felt much more manageable with her faith now in tact. Now married, she and Jason began to build a life together that was filled with hope and promise. When they found out that they were pregnant with their first child, they prepared themselves for what could come, knowing that she would be prone to experiencing postpartum depression. Emerson Chase came and brought great delight with her arrival, but the cloud of depression kept its distance. They waited, but it never came.

Confidence of victory started to fill her thoughts as she began to think that maybe, just maybe she had defeated this darkness once and for all. Maybe healing and redemption had finally come for her heart and mind.

When the news of baby #2 came, she assumed that their journey with this child would mirror their journey with their first. It did not.

Whenever there are complications surrounding a pregnancy, fear and anxiety can get the best of any of us. Left unchecked, those emotions can quickly lead to places of despair and depression. When she was put on bedrest, she still had three months of her pregnancy remaining with a toddler in tow. Being forced to lay on the couch for days on end, brought with it the unwanted feelings of loneliness that she had thought were long gone. Physically unable to perform the "expected roles" of wife and mom, she was now left with her dark, shaming thoughts. She felt so helpless, literally unable to do anything for herself and completely dependent upon others.

When the time finally came for Campbell to arrive, Taylor was determined to make up for all the time lost, or at least that's how she saw it. For the past three months, she had been unable to be anything for anyone, so now she was going to be everything for everyone. Terrified to be an additional burden, she kept trying to stand on her own strength and do everything for herself, unable to accept help from others.

She was doing far more than she should have been doing, plagued with and driven by thoughts and questions of inadequacy. "Am I enough? Will I ever be enough? Do others see me as enough?" Exhausted by this strategy to cope but not knowing any other way to get through it, she once again perfected putting on a really good face for everyone, but she was well aware of how inauthentic she was being. She was pretending, and she had gotten so good at it that she had even convinced herself that she was OK. If she could get herself to believe the lie, then maybe it would be true.

It was a dark and lonely time as she continued to push herself to her physical limits, determined to prove her worth. She was worn out. Her body ached. She was mentally drained, physically exhausted, and spiritually tapped, and she carried on this way for the first several months of Campbell's life, silently struggling and almost immune to the storm within her. She couldn't even really identify it as depression because this time, it looked so different. She had become something, someone she didn't even recognize—angry, exhausted, alone, lacking identity and purpose, and feeling trapped in a body that she no longer knew.

Her mind kept frequenting places that were dark, unhealthy, and very scary. The darkness enclosed around her with such force that she wasn't even able to turn to God in it. She couldn't pray. There were no words. She was so scared. There was so much shame attached to her struggle, shame that caused her to keep her distance even from God. Prior to this time, God was one of the first places she would go. Running to Him had become her natural default, but not now. She couldn't. She didn't even know anymore which way was up. She was drowning in despair, not even aware that it was happening.

Despite her ability to fool those around her into believing that she was doing alright, Jason saw straight through the facade into her pain. "Taylor, is this depression again?" With one simple question, her own blinders fell off, and her ability to now see things for what they really were began to set her free once again. She didn't even know what postpartum depression was, but once she started to do her research, everything made sense. She qualified for every description of it, every box was checked.

So much freedom was found in finally knowing and identifying what was happening inside of her. She suddenly felt less lonely. The daunting impossibility of every day that weighed her down began to fade. She finally understood that most of what she was feeling was beyond what she was capable of handling on her own. So much time and energy had been spent not needing God or others. It was a lightbulb moment for her faith. We were never meant to walk through this life alone. We weren't created that way. We were wired for community, for shouldering each other's burdens and doing life together. For the first time in her struggle with depression, she realized that everything she had been through was intended to point her heart toward God and her need for Him.

The next several months were filled with many small steps of faith in the same direction, slowly but surely leading her back into the arms of a loving, faithful, and good God. As she surrendered her instinct to control, fight, resist, and repress what she was feeling, she was able to get to the other side of the despair. Instead of ignoring the darkness, she faced it, but she didn't face it alone.

> *Be strong and courageous. Do not be afraid or terrified because of them, for the Lord your God goes with you; He will never leave you nor forsake you.*
>
> Deuteronomy 31:6

She clung to these words. They were life and breath to her soul. All that once held her captive in shame and fear was being replaced with faith and hope. God would not leave her. He never had, and He never would. Hope was lifting her up out of the pit.

While the struggle has not magically vanished from her life, she has been able to find herself hopeful in it and grateful for it, no longer willing to hide behind it in the shadows. She desires to bring her struggle into the light in order to help others find hope in their own suffering. Much has been learned through her years of pain and sorrow, but one truth that rises to the surface is this: Comparison is the thief of joy. Her story is no better or worse than someone else's, and to hold someone else's image above her own will only welcome her back into the pit. Paying attention to everyone else's highlight reels on social media has done her no favors. She has to daily choose to be authentic and vulnerable, knowing that this humble posture of faith will welcome hope into the wounded and hurting hearts of others.

If her story can give voice to someone else's pain, so be it. If her story can breed hope in another, she will tell it. If her story can be used for God's glory, all praise be to His name. He is worth it all. Her battle with depression has served as a constant reminder to her of her need for Jesus, and He is worth more to her than every price she has had to pay through the hurt and sorrow she has faced. She never wants to stop needing Him, and if this present struggle is what it takes to keep her desperate for Him, then let it remain.

She now sees her circumstances through the lens of hope, a perspective that allows her to see her struggle as an opportunity to help others find hope. It's given her eyes of sensitivity and compassion toward women, and in particular, moms. She is all too familiar with the battle of silently struggling, and she doesn't want women to fight alone anymore. God keeps bringing her opportunities to share her story, and she sees it as God redeeming her brokenness. There is a God who loves them, too. There is a God who can give them the strength to endure, too.

There is hope and purpose in the brokenness of her story. This is her dust, but God makes beautiful things out of the dust. The weight of it is not lost on her, but she is thankful that it continues to resurface in her life to remind her to keep coming back to the Lord, her Rock. The same strength that raised Jesus from the grave is the same strength that she has access to every single day. That is all that she needs. He won't forsake her. He has lifted her up from the pit, and He's allowed her to go back into it again and again. Still, He remains. She never felt like she was enough, but God's constant word to her was that she is more than enough in Him. Depression has allowed her to rise, to rise to every occasion to display His glory through her pain. Hope rises. God is redeeming her darkness. Hope knows no bounds.

CHAPTER 10

HOPE WAITS

Therefore, I urge you, brothers and sisters, in view of God's mercy, to offer your bodies as a living sacrifice, holy and pleasing to God—this is your true and proper worship.

Romans 12:1

A LIVING SACRIFICE ... this is what it means to be a Christ follower. It is a daily laying down of self to pick up the cross of Christ. It is a dying to the things of this world in order to live for the things of Heaven. This daily dying to self reveals a greater desire—an eternal one. What arrests our hearts' deepest longings and hopes? Do we live and long for that which is temporal and fades, or do we more so wait with eager anticipation for that which is yet to come?

Life is filled with unpleasant waiting. From the moment we inhale our very first breath, we are introduced to waiting. Little babies cry in impatience as they wait for their needs to be met. Children find it nearly impossible to be patient in the waiting for the joys and surprises of a Christmas morning. Youth struggle in the waiting to obtain a sense of freedom and independence that a driver's license can bring. Young adults are forced to wait through seasons of the unknown as they pursue higher education, career paths, and future mates.

Every time we achieve one of these milestones, another awaits us, and we are found in the waiting again. Life is waiting. Until we take our last breath on this earth, we will be found waiting for something. Waiting can be hard. Waiting can be long. I'd like to add to that dialogue today, though. Hope can be connected to our seasons of waiting. When we find ourselves in these holding patterns of life, hope can replace the disappointment. Hope can be the louder voice. Hope can be our reality.

We are going to spend some time together in Romans chapter 12, and as we pore over these inspired words, let's allow them to have their intended effect on our hearts. I'm a note taker—I always have been, and I probably always will be. I take notes whenever and wherever I can. Packed into the tiny margins of my Bible are countless words, phrases, dates, and thoughts that have captivated my mind and soul as I've studied God's Word. Some pages are far more marked up than others. Some pages are frequented more than others. Romans 12 in my Bible is one such page. I wish I could take a picture of it and show you exactly what I mean. I've underlined, highlighted, and scribbled much in these tiny margins of this one chapter, and I find myself returning to this chapter again and again because of the importance of its message:

Live like a follower of Jesus Christ.

If only all professing believers in all the world actually did this, this world would be a much different place. If we all understood that this life was going to be filled with waiting, and instead of resisting the waiting, we chose to be found faithful in it, I can only dream of the hope that would fill hearts. Can you imagine if the term "Christian" was actually a description by which people desired to be known? If we learned to wait well with our hope intact, there would be a world of lost souls found waiting at the foot of the cross, eager to receive the grace and redemption that we have received.

> *Do not conform to the pattern of this world, but be transformed by the renewing of your mind. Then you will be able to test and approve what God's will is—His good, pleasing and perfect will.*
>
> Romans 12:2

The world does not dignify waiting. It abhors it. Nobody really wants to wait. It's not in our nature to wait well. We are impatient by default. We've been taught through our own bent toward sin and our fallen culture that we should have what we want when we want to have it. We've been told to believe that we deserve what we want and that we should not be denied that which we desire.

God's Word invites us to a better way, and the conversation of Romans 12 gives us the details. Live sacrificially and allow the truth of God to transform the way you think. Live in such a way that your desires are held loosely in open hands before the Lord, knowing that God is good and faithful in all that He does. When we face trials and all kinds of tribulations, God is good and faithful. When we are forced to wait longer than we'd like to, God is good and faithful. When our prayers appear to go unheard or unanswered, God is good and faithful. Our seasons of waiting do not translate into God's inability to be on time. God is never late. Hope waits through the affliction, through the unmet longings, through the ongoing desires, because hope knows that Jesus is worth every minute of the wait.

It is hard to live like a follower of Jesus in a world that does not honor such a way of life. This world upholds fame, fortune, power, and prestige. This world honors position and status. This world prioritizes pleasure and self-gratification. None of those things matter in God's economy. When we bring ourselves to a place in our faith where we can surrender our desire for that which this world esteems, the waiting becomes a lighter load to bear. When we stop elevating created things over the Creator, perspectives shift and hope abounds.

> *For by the grace given me I say to every one of you: Do not think of yourself more highly than you ought, but rather think of yourself with sober judgment, in accordance with the faith God has distributed to each of you.*
>
> Romans 12:3

Hope and humility seem to go hand in hand. To keep our hope in seasons of waiting, it seems paramount that we also see ourselves through an accurate lens. We are sinners saved by grace. We are broken vessels who have been restored. We are never beyond the need of God's mercy, and we are also never without the power of His Spirit. If we are ever going to wait well, we must be found in complete and utter dependence upon the strength that only He can provide, and this supernatural provision comes in the form of specific gifts that He has given to each one of us.

Romans 12 goes on to list some of the many gifts that have been given to us in Christ: gifts of service, teaching, exhortation, generosity, leadership, and mercy, just to mention a few. We have been supernaturally gifted to live like Jesus. The power that accompanies these gifts enables us to live a victorious, Christian life. It allows our love for others to be genuine when the love of this world is so often inauthentic and counterfeit. It equips us to cling to that which is good when this world keeps running after evil. It empowers us to honor one another instead of trying to outdo one another. This power ignites our zeal and motivates our passion to serve the Lord, so that we can …

> *Be joyful in hope, patient in affliction,*
> *faithful in prayer.*
>
> **Romans 12:12**

At the center of hope, there is waiting. Because hope is a strong and confident expectation of what is to come, waiting is assumed within its very essence. Isn't it interesting, then, that it is possible to be joyful in our hope? Hope waits with joy, with eager expectancy and anticipation, because hope knows the end of the story. Hope is confident that what is yet to come will far surpass the greatest joys of what is now. Hope knows that the hardship of today is momentary in comparison to the glory that will be revealed one day. As hope patiently waits through affliction and trial, hope increases, because hope knows no bounds.

Romans 12:12 was written to a group of faithful believers

who were surrounded on every side by perversion, evil, godlessness, and the threat of persecution. The imperative of verse 12 was not missed on Paul, the one who wrote these words, and it certainly was not missed on the Roman Christians, the ones who first read these words. In faith, Paul commanded them to be joyful as they waited in their hope. He commanded them to be patient in the affliction that kept coming their way. He commanded them to be faithful in prayer, knowing that uninterrupted communion with God in prayer would be a catalyst in securing their hope. The Roman believers received these words like a breath of fresh air, grateful for these commands, and willing to walk in obedience to them.

Through the foreknowledge of God and the inspiration of the Holy Spirit, these words ring just as strong and true for us today. These three imperatives are meant to be the noticeable markings of every follower of Jesus Christ. Are they? Do we receive these commands with such eagerness and joy as the original recipients did? No matter the season of waiting in which you find yourself today, you were called to be joyful in hope. No matter the longing you carry in your heart that awaits fulfillment, you were called to be patient in affliction. No matter the length of the wait in which you find yourself, you were called to be faithful in prayer. Obedience to these three commands is crucial for hope to be had and maintained in our lives.

The command is not to cease hoping for that which you desire. Just hope for Jesus more. Long for Jesus more. Desire Jesus more than all other things, even good things. We were created with God-given desires, dreams, and longings. Each one of those things was meant to point us toward the Creator, though. Each one of those things was meant to reveal to us an even greater need and deeper longing than temporary things could ever provide. Hope waits through the pain and waits on the promise to come. God isn't finished writing your story yet, and He isn't finished with Cassie's either.

This is her hope story.

Waiting has been a theme, an almost constant thread woven throughout Cassie's story. She has been found in expectant seasons of waiting, and in painful ones, as well. Waiting has proven to be both difficult and rewarding in her life. Even today, she remains in another season of waiting, but she has come to learn that hope waits on the Lord.

Like many young girls, she had always dreamed of the day when she would be a wife and a mom. It was just assumed in her heart that she would live what she considered to be the normal life and fulfill the dreams of her heart's deepest desires. Never would she have imagined that she would reach the age of 30 as a single woman. Her mother had married young. Her sister had followed suit. Many of her friends had found love while in their early 20s. Why wouldn't she, too?

We were created with the desire to love and to be loved fully in return. We were made for relationship—first with Jesus, and then with others. Cassie knew this to be true, but while marriage and motherhood were strong desires, she was never really consumed with the desire to date. Her high school years were spent single, but they were joyful years, nonetheless. Her college years didn't look much different. No one really caught her eye, and she wasn't about to waste her heart on just anyone. She had learned to develop good friendships with guys, but she was reserving her heart for someone who would care for it well.

Love entered her life when she was 20 years old, in the form of her first serious relationship. They loved each other. They told each other how much they loved each other. It was easy for her to envision her future with this man as their love continued to grow. She dreamed about their wedding day—the dress, the flowers, the vows, the rings, the kiss. In her mind, it was only a matter of time. He had told her everything she had waited a lifetime to hear from a man. He had committed himself to her. Her heart rested in his hands.

"The tongue has the power of life and death," Proverbs 18:21 says. Words have a way of wounding a heart like few other things can. Promises broken have the ability to shatter hope. "Cassie, I don't love you anymore. I don't want to be with you. This is over." With no warning and even less tact, his words cut her heart in two. How could this be over when she had put so much hope in this relationship? How could he change his mind so suddenly when they had just been talking about marriage and a life of forever together? How could he be so heartless? While she had been dreaming of their future, he had been dating someone else. His heart was already in someone else's hands while her heart fell to the ground, shattered into pieces.

This brokenness lingered as she began to pursue other opportunities, always the background noise to the soundtrack of her life. Just after her sophomore year of college, she went to Spain on a short-term missions trip, and once again fell in love, but this time with the culture and the ministry that she worked with there. A newfound love for serving God began to awaken something inside of her, something that had lain dormant for quite some time. She wanted her life to have a greater purpose than that which she had known. She wanted her life to matter. These two short weeks had done something inside of her, and her appetite was whet for more.

Months later, she packed her bags and returned to Spain, this time for six months. Ministry consumed her days, and joy was once again beginning to spring up within her heart. As the days and weeks turned into months, she spent much time reflecting on the loss of her relationship and how it had impacted her faith. Time spent far removed from her normal, everyday life was proving to be incredibly beneficial for her growth in the Lord and exactly what she needed to heal.

She was beginning to see so much more clearly now how much she had gained through that painful loss. Her ministry in Spain wouldn't have been a part of her life if that relationship would have ended in marriage. Her faith was growing stronger every day, and these six months were challenging her to grow in ways she never could have imagined. It was a life-giving and life-changing season of new hope and new beginnings.

When she returned home from her time in Spain, she just seemed to pick things back up right where she had left them. She went back to her old job, back to her old friends, back to her old ministry—a different person trying to fit back into her old life, a life that had changed. While not all of this returning was bad, in some ways it was beginning to feel as if she had never left—that all the growth and change had happened to someone else. Not really knowing how to bring back with her all that she experienced in Spain, she set out to merge these two lives together.

A life of busyness became her new normal, but she

was getting lost in the noise of it all. She said "yes" to everything, desperately trying to figure out where she belonged, where she fit best. Her time in Spain had been so transformational. She had grown so passionate about serving the Lord there. Now back in the States, she found herself in a dry, desert-like place, weary and tired from constant activity that offered little joy. She was just waiting … waiting to find her purpose, waiting to find the one with whom she would share her life, waiting on God to show up here just like He had there.

This season of waiting continued for a few more years. Throughout this time, her walk with the Lord was filled with both mountain tops and valleys, highs and lows, and seasons of obedience that were both passionless and passion filled. Still, she kept pressing on in the waiting, confident that God knew what He was doing, even if He hadn't shared those plans with her yet. Years of faithfully serving in volunteer roles at her church led to an opportunity for her to join the staff there as a part-time employee, an opportunity that she gladly accepted. Hopes of finding purpose and worth ignited again within her heart as she continued to wait on the Lord to reveal His plans for her in this new season.

The promises of God are often revealed and realized in our lives in some of the most unexpected ways. We spend years dreaming and praying about one thing while God is often busy working out something quite different, always knowing what is best for us, always operating within His perfect timing. While on staff at her church, God began to bring clarity to another dream Cassie had held onto for quite some time, and she watched with hope-filled joy as this dream started to materialize. As she and her sister partnered together in business to own and run their own bakery, Cassie once again began to see how God was always working out the details of her life in ways she could never have imagined.

Success has marked their business endeavor, and there has been so much joy along the way as she has been able to do what she loves with one of the people she loves most in this life, her sister. Still, there is an ache that accompanies this journey, too. Her sister is happily married to the man of her dreams, getting to partner with him in this business. Cassie stills waits for her dream of marriage to be fulfilled. She doesn't love her job any less. She just wants to be able to share the joys of it with someone else, a husband. So, she remains in a season of waiting.

As the years of waiting have endured, so has her faith in the face of her hopes being deferred. A few others have come and gone—friendships she had hoped would become much more—but things have continued to not turn out as she had hoped. Marriage and motherhood remain strong, deeply-rooted desires in her heart, but through the painful seasons of waiting, her hope has become secure. She has made a steadfast decision in her waiting. She has shifted her focus from her unmet desires of a relationship with a man to her relationship with the Lord.

This shift of perspective has opened her eyes to see the goodness of the Lord in her life right now. So many of her dreams have been fulfilled in ways she would have never imagined—dreams that may have never been realized in her life if her greatest dream would have been fulfilled in her initial, desired timing. Every step forward in the waiting has proven to increase her trust in the One who is calling. Every step toward Him has been a step worth taking, and the further she walks with the Lover of her soul, the further she desires to go.

So, she continues to wait on the Lord. There have been seasons of her life when the singleness has tasted very bitter, and there have been times when it has been so sweet. Invitations to weddings and baby showers often serve to remind her of all that she continues to wait for. Some days, she loathes being single. Other days, she embraces the blessing of it. There are days when her questions seem to shout louder than her hope. "Ok God, where are you in this?" Then, there are days of fullness that follow those hard days—days that are filled with a deeper sense of completion and purpose that her singleness provides.

Is she still lonely at times? Of course, she is. Does she still want marriage and a family? Absolutely, she does, but she's learning to find joy in this part of her journey, too. When she was younger, she clung to wishes which she assumed were hope. Happiness would come when her wishes were fulfilled. Now, through faith and maturity, she knows that she can rely on the promises of God and that He will provide for her every need. It may not be the way she would choose or the way her 15 year old heart would have thought, but her hope is in this unwavering trust: God is faithful and He keeps His promises. Her hope is no longer placed in a desired outcome but in the promise-giver.

While she continues to wait on what her future will look like, she finds herself in another season of waiting in her business and waiting on what the fullness of that will look like. Among the many lessons learned, Cassie knows now that instant gratification is not where the promise is found. Waiting has been a theme in her life, and it will more than likely prove to be a lifelong journey. She sees the long-term plans and the things she desires, but she's learning to trust those to God and the outcomes to His control.

Hope has been found in the waiting. Waiting is not reserved for singles or any other specific demographic. All people can be found in seasons of waiting, and she is learning to be found faithful in hers. The heaviness of waiting can be made lighter as that burden is shared with others, so Cassie shares her story of hope. The waiting has helped fuel her obedience to the Lord. She knows His Word tells her to be constant in prayer, so she remains constant in prayer over the desires of her heart, and treasure has emerged from the dry, desert places. God's voice has become clear, and she is learning to listen to Him as He speaks. "Cassie, say yes to scary things." So, in faith, she has continued to step outside of her comfort zone, and she has been met with wonder in the unknown. Confident that God will continue to use every valley and every height for His glory and for her good, her hope waits.

Made in the USA
San Bernardino, CA
19 January 2018